Infinite Existence

Indomitable Spirit • Limitless Potential

Co-create One's Conscious Reality
on Country, Earth and in the Universe

FIRST PRINCIPLE – FIRST NATIONS ACKNOWLEDGEMENT

It is with a deep sense of gratitude One acknowledges and recognises the First Nations peoples of the world as the traditional custodians of Country (land, sea* and sky) on Earth. One openly, generously and humbly offers One's respect to First Nations peoples' living cultures, affirms One's special connection to place and celebrates One's adaptive, vibrant communities, as well as One's spiritual ancestors and Elders past, present and emerging. One honours the spirit in One and all sentient Beings on the planet and in the universe.

*Throughout this book, all references to 'sea' include all bodies of water.

Everything is connected – All is One

First published in Australia in 2022 by:
Shawn Wondunna-Foley
Innerway
PO Box 2141
Hervey Bay QLD 4655
Australia
www.innerway.com.au

Copyright © Shawn Wondunna-Foley 2022

All rights reserved. This book is copyright. Apart from any fair dealings for the purposes of private study, research, criticism or review permitted under the Australian Copyright Act 1968, no part may be stored or reproduced by any process without prior written permission. Enquiries should be made to the publisher.

ISBN: 978-0-646-84866-2

 A catalogue record for this book is available from the National Library of Australia

Front cover design: Lorna Hendry and Shawn Wondunna-Foley
Editing and layout: Lorna Hendry
Typeset in A-Space and Born
Printing: IngramSpark

INFINITE EXISTENCE

Indomitable Spirit • Limitless Potential

Co-create One's Conscious Reality
on Country, Earth and in the Universe

Shawn Wondunna-Foley

Disclaimer

The information contained in this book is for general guidance on matters of spiritual enlightenment and mindful living interest only. While the author has made every attempt to ensure that the quotes and information contained within this book have been obtained from reliable sources and are correct at the time of printing, the author and the publisher are not responsible for any errors or omissions or for the results obtained from the use of this information. All information in this book is provided 'as is', with no guarantee of completeness, accuracy or timeliness, or of the results obtained from the use of this information, and without warranty of any kind, expressed or implied, including, but not limited to, warranties of performance, merchantability and fitness for a particular purpose. In no event will the author or publisher, its partnerships or corporations or the partners agents or employees thereof be liable to you or anyone else for any decision made or action taken in reliance on the information in this book or for any consequential, special or similar damages, even if advised of the possibility of such damages.

About the author

Butchulla (*Badtjala*) First Nation Australian independent author, Shawn Wondunna-Foley is a public speaker, positive thought leader, streetscape/visual/installation artist, creative designer, spiritual lifestyle coach, cultural advisor and ideas-wellness philanthropist. Currently working as a public servant, Shawn has a great love of Country (land, sea and sky). He values the arts, culture and the community (Hervey Bay) where he lives, works and plays on the Fraser Coast in regional Queensland, Australia.

Shawn is the author of two cultural heritage publications – *The Badtjala People, I on Country* – as well as mindfulness and spiritual consciousness books on wellness and wellbeing – *One, Two* and *Three*. His self-published quotes book, *One*, was sold out twice and the series continues to be a fantastic resource and awesome gift for people seeking inner guidance and a more enlightened inner way to live One's life in this modern world on Earth.

Recently, Shawn released his first major nonfiction work, *Awaken: Co-create the best version of oneself now*. Its benefits are now gently rippling out into the world like a global thought wave of inner change, realisation and awakening for all who have read it.

Shawn acknowledges and aligns with the universal idea: 'Everything is Connected – All is One'. Everyone is spiritually entangled in an ocean of conscious existence with all other sentient Beings in the universe.

Infinite Existence is Shawn's second major nonfiction work. It is an inner journey of spiritual awareness and wakeful living presence on Country (land, sea and sky), Earth, in the solar system and this galaxy.

Read Shawn's blog and connect with him on his website www.innerway.com.au. One is also invited to click on the resources at www.innerway.com.au, which supports this book and his learning, teachings and pointings.

> First Nations peoples have always had an intimate knowing and intangible connection to spirit. It is something that lives within everyone and Country (land, sea and sky). To live without spirit is like trying to breathe without air.
> – Shawn Wondunna-Foley

Dedication

Space and time may appear to separate the shared oneness between oneself and all who read this book. But it is only an illusion of One's human senses. One's spirit, soul or cosmic consciousness reaches out across this vast universe to One 'now'.

One extends One's 'spiritual heart' and invites One to experience a new way to perceive, ponder and prosper in the world. Ultimately, One's way in life is to live in divine alignment with the universe. There is no greater opportunity than transcending One's egoic mindset and becoming something truly amazing in One's lifetime.

This book is dedicated to everyone who has ever sensed, sought or seeks to know how to co-create and experience a new living wellness and positive wellbeing in One's life. Living well is an expression of One's conscious manifested reality on Earth. The way to One's inner peace and wakeful living presence in life begins the moment One looks inside oneself. Dare to seek the truth and One will surely find it now.

One aims to inspire One to embrace seven key universal virtues, seven key spiritual truths, One's infinite existence and become a 'Bright' – an awake spirit of divine light, love, oneness and compassion. Through the natural alignment of mind, body and spirit with 'the way' of the universe, One will realise One's awakened consciousness within oneself.

Wherever One is on Earth, this book serves as a 'spiritual guide to the universe' for One's inner realisation and awakening in the world.

The first step in knowing One's divine spirit, soul or cosmic consciousness is to realise One's infinite existence in the universe. The second is to simply co-create a space for this inner journey of awakening to manifest in One's life now. Know that the right moment always happens at the right time and in the right way. The chapters in this book will expand One's spiritual awareness, enhance One's transformation process, and improve One's intuitive intelligence. One's desire for a deeper and intimate knowing of One's infinite existence, life and the universe will be nurtured and nourished within oneself.

Divine synchronicity is 'the way' of the universe; this is how it self-organises everything, without ever doing anything, so that all things are done.

Imbued within the silence of every page that One turns in this book is a special message of infinite light, love, and oneness to all sentient Beings. The universe is truly a magical and amazing creation for One and all.

One spirit – One way – One universe.

Shawn Wondunna-Foley
Hervey Bay, Queensland, Australia

BE ONE NOW

One simple moment of spiritual realisation.
One divine awakening for all of humankind.

Shawn Wondunna-Foley

Contents

Important note: Language of Spirit or 'One'........................2

Living Presence..4

Useful Terms 6

Freedom 10

Introduction..11

Chapter 1. Spirit...37
Divinity Within One

Chapter 2. Knowing..69
One's Divine Spirit

Chapter 3. The Way 97
Align With Spirit, Country and the Universe

Chapter 4. Co-existence......................................125
Manifesting Conscious Experiences

Chapter 5. Change..165
Evolving as a Spiritual Being

Chapter 6. Reality 191
Conscious Choice to be Free

Chapter 7. Inspiration.......................................223
Action Without Expectation

Acknowledgements 257

Endnote...259

Important note: Language of Spirit or 'One'

Throughout the pages of this book, a new language of spirit or 'One' has been used and incorporated to enable the reader to realise a new way of perceiving, thinking, feeling, living and being in the world today.

The Sapir-Whorf hypothesis of linguistic relativity states that the language One speaks influences, limits and determines how One sees or perceives One's world and the universe. This book is written in an English 'spiritual language style', which uses the term 'One'. It reflects a non-dimensional and non-linear view of space-time. Every spiritual thought takes the form beginning with, or inclusive of, 'One', where 'One' is spirit, soul or cosmic consciousness.

'One' is an inclusive term referring to spirit, soul, cosmic consciousness, Source, the Creator, God, Allah or Divine Supreme Being. It has been written in this way to reflect an intimate conversation between the spiritual Source for all things in the universe and One's spirit.

The terms 'I', 'you' and 'your' have been deliberately omitted in order to provide greater clarity, spiritual unity and global inclusiveness. This distinction is key and fundamental in shifting One's mindful perception to a more profound inner knowing and divine sense of oneness within One's spirit or Being. It is about intentionally and purposely co-creating a space with 'no self' to know oneself. To undertake One's ultimate spiritual journey in this life, it is best to 'remove oneself from the equation of One's life'.

Where there is no 'I', there can be only 'One'. Where there is no 'You', there can be only 'One'. In the absence of 'I', 'me', 'mine', 'you' or 'your', there is only ever One's divine spirit, soul or cosmic consciousness. This is One's eternal presence in the universe. One has co-created this new language and the opportunity to inspire One's way of living and being through One's realisation and awakening of One's spiritual truth – here and now. Know that there is no space or distance between oneself and One's spirit. When One looks inwards, One will know One's inner way and direction in life.

There has never been a more perfect moment in One's life to journey deeply within oneself and awaken to One's own divine existence and living reality on Earth. All that ever was and will ever be in the universe is present within One's infinite divine presence 'Now'. Wherever One goes on planet Earth, or in any other part of the known universe, One is already home – Be Here Now.

> Be the divine truth within oneself and One's spiritual vision will be able to see through the illusion of chaos in this life.
> – Shawn Wondunna-Foley

Living Presence

Greetings dear spiritual traveller. As One undertakes One's journey across the universe, One welcomes One here to this moment now.

Although One has never met and will most likely never meet in person, there is a reason that One has found this book. Take this as a sign from the universe that One is on the right path. Know that things will get better, everything will be alright and One will always get through whatever is troubling One today. Take two deep, long breaths and exhale slowly so One can simply relax. It is time to release any fears or stress, let go and unwind. Remember that One is important, One's existence is valid and One is right where One needs to be. One is stronger than One realises or knows at this moment in time. One is still here and co-creating a better version of oneself each day. One's efforts to make things better on Earth matter. So does aspiring to live a better life that will benefit One and all other sentient Beings now.

One is grateful and gives thanks for living on this beautiful planet. One is not alone in this world or universe. One hopes this message inspires and encourages One to consciously co-create a new reality on Country, Earth and in the Universe. What One seeks is also searching for One too. Being here now is knowing that One's life is purposeful and on a divine inner path. One's consciousness is expanding in a way that is raising One's vibrations to align with One's higher spiritual self. One's inner awareness is the key to transforming One's life into an awakened state of existence.

The world is a wonderful place full of good-hearted, kind and loving people with pure divine spirits, souls or cosmic consciousnesses. When the collective consciousness of humans living on the planet unites in the deep knowing that all is truly One, then an amazing transformation of the world will have begun to happen towards a spiritually based Type 1 civilisation on Earth. Everything that humanity has been striving for is potentially present within all people. Nothing can change this divine path of spiritual evolution or destroy the deepest feelings of great joy, love and oneness within One for all of humankind.

'The way' home to a new Earth and new future already exists within each and every sentient Being on Earth. Together, let us align in synchronicity to manifest it now.

Useful Terms

Bright
An enlightened awake spiritual sentient Being.

co-existence theory of the universe
Where all dimensional matter-energy (altered consciousness) and non-dimensional states (consciousness) or field-states co-exist relative to each other. A theory of everything that describes the coherence of all separate theories into a single theory of co-existence within the universe. This theory gives rise to a singularity of infinite existence in the universe.

infinite state theory of spiritual consciousness
A way of predicting the probabilities of a sentient Being existing in one or all seven infinite states of consciousness. As a sentient Being of multi non-dimensional conscious states, One exists in a single state and all states simultaneously (i.e. the eighth state). Until a particular state of spiritual consciousness is aligned within a sentient Being, One exists as an expression of all states of consciousness at the same time.

infinite existence equation
The probability of a Being's state of consciousness is determined by the square of One's consciousness, which is represented here by the omega symbol (Ω) from the Greek alphabet. One's infinite existence in the universe can be represented by the following equation:

$$\text{Infinite Existence} = \text{Infinity} \times \text{Consciousness}^2$$
$$IE = \infty \times \Omega^2$$

insanity
The state of being a sane person who tries repeatedly to 'fit' into a world where most people have uploaded a stream of egoic unconscious mindless memes or thoughts into One's human mind's living operating system.

light hole
A state of non-dimensional existence that has an infinite presence of Source Consciousness so intense that all spiritual consciousness is drawn to it.

meme
An element of a culture or system of behaviour passed from one individual to another by imitation or other non-genetic means. Also an image, video or piece of text, typically humorous in nature, that is copied and spread rapidly by internet users, often with slight variations.

quantum consciousness
A state of existence or 'isness' where quantum mechanics and spiritual consciousness are indistinguishable from one state or the other and where the probability of a non-duality or singularity exists as it is observed or manifested.

sacred space
An embodied emptiness by a particular individual within One's mind–body–spirit holding a great respect, openness and alignment to co-create a new manifested reality or experience.

self-organising theory
The capacity of a system to change itself by creating new structures, adding new negative and positive feedback loops, promoting new information flows and making new rules. It is a process where the organisation (constraint, redundancy) of a system spontaneously increases, without this increase being controlled by the environment or an encompassing or otherwise external system.

seven key states of consciousness
Knowing, awareness, oneness, joy, free will, peace and presence.

seven key virtues
Compassion, helpfulness, acceptance, simplicity, patience, generosity and openness.

sol
A solar day on Earth. The interval between two successive returns of the Sun to the same meridian (sundial time) as seen by an observer on Earth.

statum intuitanics
Within consciousness where One is in alignment with One's state-based knowing, sensing, or understanding by intuition and/or intuitive spiritual intelligence.

spiritual entanglement
A phenomenon where Source Consciousness is present in such a way that the individual spiritual states of consciousness exist independently until aligned, and the act of conscious alignment of one influences the other, even at a distance from each other in space-time within the universe.

spiritual singularity
A state of non-dimensional conscious reality where states of consciousness exist in infinite or endless beingness.

spiritual sovereignty
A state of self-awareness and self-realisation about One's true spiritual nature as a divine spirit who has infinite existence in the universe and takes full self-responsibility for One's life. The act of freely declaring 'One is Spirit', 'One is Free Now'.

the way
A term used in Buddhism or Zen teachings that, in its simplest definition, means an approach to life that flows in harmony and alignment with nature or the natural synergy of the universe in the present moment.

Type 1 civilisation
The Kardashev scale categorises a civilisation's level of technological advancement based on the amount of energy it is able to use:

- a Type 1 civilisation can use and store all of the energy available on its planet
- a Type 2 civilisation can use and control energy at the scale of its planetary system
- a Type 3 civilisation can control energy at the scale of its entire host galaxy.

A Type 1 civilisation has been able to harness all the energy that is available from a neighbouring star, gathering and storing it to meet the energy demands and needs of the population.

Freedom

Freedom is walking in silence at dawn
Freedom is breathing with quiet pause
Freedom is blossoms flowering in the sun
Freedom is eagles feeding fish to young

Freedom is sunlight, sea waves and sand
Freedom is moments holding One's hand
Freedom is the night and sparkling stars above
Freedom is the way One unconditionally loves

Freedom is nature doing what must be done
Freedom is laughter, joyful tears and fun
Freedom is letting go of all that appears
Freedom is believing spirit, not ego's fears

Freedom is the simplicity of life itself
Freedom is being present not anywhere else
Freedom is an experience of living One's life
Freedom is aligning mind–body–spirit right

Shawn Wondunna-Foley

Introduction

During the visit of Their Royal Highnesses, the Duke and Duchess of Sussex (Harry and Meghan) to K'gari (Fraser Island) in late 2018, the idea of this book first began to arise within One.

As One walked with His Royal Highness on the white sandy shoreline of Boorangoora (Lake McKenzie), enjoying the fresh water at One's feet and the cool gentle breeze blowing across the surface of the lake, a moment of realisation occurred to One.

What if One could bring One's deep sense of love for spirit, Country (land, sea and sky) and way of being to all?

Emerging from this moment was a creative desire and inspiration to share the wisdom of One's inner spirit and way of being with the world from a very personal and authentic space. A conversation that would cut through the clutter and confusion of contemporary life and speak directly to One's heart about spirit from a personal perspective and firsthand experiences.

One knew that time would pass as effortlessly as the sun travelling across the sky or fresh water flowing out to the ocean, no matter whatever One chooses to do or not do. So, with this in mind, One started to think about and imagine what this book may look like when finished. The more One thought about it, the more One's mind-body vibrated with creative excitement about the idea of writing this book.

Like an early morning mist rising silently above the perched lakes on K'gari, an image of this book began to slowly appear. One appreciates that manifesting any great idea or inspiring thought takes time, as well as unconditional love, patience, cooperation and commitment. So too this writing project would require One's ongoing mindful attention and spiritual presence.

Great people do not fear time nor projects of significance. One only sees an opportunity to manifest One's vision, like flowing along an endless river to One's final destination, desired dream or realised reality.

With One's vision in mind, One created managed spaces in One's life to converse with the pristine part of One's spirit and moments to align with the purity of divine oneness in the universe. To think of it in a simpler way, One decided to just let go, which allowed One to trust in the process and the silence of divine wisdom to speak through One's spirit and onto the pages of this book. Thankfully it all worked out in the end – phew! (Breathing a great sigh of relief and heartfelt blessing for the journey of this book.)

Throughout the creative writing process, One needed to revisit some key principles in regard to being flexible and flowing with the divine way of the universe. Essentially, this meant being aware that all things happen when they need to happen and that everything occurs right on time.

One was comfortable and content in knowing that there is nothing One can do to change 'the way' of the universe – so One chose to accept it completely. Everything moves in sync with a natural divine rhythm of this world which is always in balance and harmony. One simply enjoys what life offers, knowing that One's mind–body needs will be fulfilled as surely as the tide flows in.

Writing this book has been a journey of loving inspiration, divine alignment and transforming experience for One. When One began this process, One was unaware of how the words would flow and form on the pages, but within One's mind and spirit was an undeniable belief and divine presence of One's spirit to bring this inner voice to life and share this gift with others on the planet. In creating this book, One encourages all to be as excited reading it as when One was writing it.

Like a bright star in the night sky, may this book be a light to guide One on One's life journey.

This is the right time to open One's spirit (heart-centre or heart chakra) and mind to embrace this new and unique opportunity to enable One to explore and celebrate One's inner spirit and divine destiny in life – here and now. As One holds this book in One's hands or reads it on an electronic device, know that there is no illusion strong enough in One's mind that can hide oneself from One's spirit and the truth.

One is often drawn to the following thought about time, space and living in the now, which One has adapted from Asha Tyson, an American author and motivational speaker:

> One's journey has moulded oneself for One's greater good. And it is exactly what it needed to be. Do not think for one moment that One has lost any time. It took each and every moment One has encountered to bring One to the now. And now is right on time.

Throughout 2022, One returned to complete the manuscript for the book. This involved revising, reworking and refocusing the concept and design of the book in various ways. As part of this process, One looked at the overall concept, feel-good approach and what would best suit One's individual style, speaking voice and be of most benefit to the readers.

During the day, One worked full-time managing Queensland Government contracts to assist vulnerable people in the community through investments and partnerships with non-government agencies, organisations and suppliers. This only allowed for short windows of time in the morning, evenings or on weekends where One could dedicate oneself to the creative writing process. This was where One was able to dedicate a significant amount of time to simply meditate and write mindfully with purposeful spiritual intent. Eventually, One was able to complete the planned writing schedule ahead of time. This was a great blessing in One's life. One was so grateful for the time, space and freedom just to write.

After the COVID-19 pandemic, One had a great sense of knowing, inner joy and belief that the universe was on One's side. Everything was going to be okay, no matter whatever happened. It would all pass. This is exactly what One kept reminding oneself along the way.

The best time One found to write was after meditating or when One's mind was clear, open and empty of any and all distracting thoughts. Sometimes this would be following an early morning walk along the beach in Hervey Bay or early in the evening.

Upon reflection, One discovered that when One's mind–body–spirit was in alignment with the oneness of the universe, words flowed effortlessly onto the pages of this book like a freshwater stream on K'gari flowing to the ocean. When One creates space for spirit in One's life, One naturally nurtures an oasis of spiritual sanctuary within oneself too.

Thich Nhat Hanh, a Vietnamese Buddhist monk, teacher, author, poet and peace activist says:

> At any moment, you have a choice, that either leads you closer to your spirit or further away from it.

This book is a standing invitation to journey along an inner way to One's spirit and align with it and the universe now.

Gautama Buddha, also known as Siddhārtha Gautama, Shakyamuni Buddha, or simply 'the Buddha', was a monk, mendicant and sage who lived and taught mostly in the north-eastern part of ancient India sometime between the 6th and 4th centuries BCE, and whose inspirational teachings founded Buddhism, says:

> No One saves us but ourselves. No One can and no One may. We ourselves must walk the path.

Know that since the beginning of humanity, One has always co-created and manifested whatever thoughts and beliefs were held within or continually occupied the majority of One's mind.

Buddha also knew this about humanity, and says:

> With our thoughts we make the world.

People have been co-creating, reshaping and reconfiguring the world since the dawn of humanity from a place within One's mind. Countless people, First Nations, empires and civilisations have all come and gone over time – the only constant in the universe is change.

Upon reflection of One's life journey on this planet, One has always had a slightly altered perspective or feeling of misalignment within One's mind–body–spirit about the so-called 'truths' of learning/culture/society and the projected expectations of the people in the community to believe and behave in a certain way. Ever since One was a young boy growing up in the coastal town (now city) of Hervey Bay in Queensland, Australia, One had an inquisitive, creative and adventurous mind. Later in One's early childhood, aged about nine, One's family moved to Sydney, a major city on the east coast of Australia, to continue One's education through the later part of One's primary school years and then into high school at Asquith Boys High School. One could always remember looking at things slightly differently and being confused by the spoken words and mismatched actions of people in daily life. One would often make a mental note in One's mind about the pretence of care and concern that other people had and at the same time also hold an outward silence of inaction, particularly to First Nations peoples in Australia. On the face of it, these people appeared to be compliant, accepting things on face value as things were and not questioning any social injustices in the community, state, territory or country of Australia at the time. However, in One's simplistic way, One guessed that it was easier for most people to just get along and go about their daily tasks and activities without ever having any real honest conversations or discussions regarding the deeper and more fundamental questions about life, existence and the universe. This silence is echoed deeply in all aspects of Australian society and still exists today. It is a silence that does not speak to the injustices of the past or the present. It is an intergenerational stain on the pages of prosperity that people write One's present-day lives upon.

As One was growing up, One would often think about, reflect upon and ask those normal psycho-social self-identity questions of oneself such as:

- Who am 'I'?
- Where do 'I' fit or belong?
- What is the purpose, direction and meaning of this life and living it?

These are fundamental human identity questions that One carried within oneself and returned to time and time again in moments of silence and quietness throughout One's life. Nothing new there – these questions are basic and universal human questions that One normally asks about One's inner Being, living experiences and life on Earth.

It wasn't until much later in life that One changed the questions to:

- Who is One?
- What is One's purpose here and now?

This ignited a spiritual paradigm shift in One's living consciousness and mindful presence on Earth.

One attributes this inner quest for a 'universal truth' and knowing in part to how One's parents managed the family culture of relating to each other, other people and the natural landscape. One's thinking, behaviours and direction of self-discovery and inner exploration were significantly influenced by One's participation in family life and family activities. One's parent's cultural lineages were from two distinctly different worlds. One's mother was a dark brown-skinned Butchulla (*Badtjala*) First Nation Australian Aboriginal woman belonging to K'gari (Fraser Island) and the Fraser Coast, Queensland, Australia and One's father's lineage was from Ireland – first-generation Irish Australian. An interesting mix to say the least, especially at the time of their marriage, in the early 1960s, in a country where inter-racial marriages were socially frowned upon and in most cases barely tolerated by the governing 'white' authorities of the day, communities and society. This is why One's mum and dad got married in Western Australia, as far away from Queensland as possible, after touring Australia together.

One grew up with a deep questioning of things, social norms, challenging the status-quo/authority/administration, as well as being impacted by perceptions of others in the community, including, for a brief time, living under and subject to the Queensland Government's more infamous pieces of legislation, the *Aboriginals Protection and Restriction of the Sale of Opium Act 1897 (Qld)*. One notes with concern that One's mother was subject to this Act since birth and for a considerable period of her life in Queensland. It had a profound impact on One's mother's decision-making processes and life choices. It is noted in the Queensland State Archives that this Act created the positions of Protectors of Aboriginals, and in 1904, the Office of the Chief Protector of Aboriginals. Although presented at the time as a charitable, humane and philanthropic measure, the Act in its practical outcome was oppressive and restricted the freedom of Aboriginal people more effectively than it did the sale of opium. The 1897 Act and the subsequent Amendment Acts up until 1946 gave the Chief Protector of Aboriginals, as well as the individual Protectors, enormous control over almost all aspects of the lives of Aboriginal and Torres Strait Islander people in Queensland. The legislation was used to control thousands of Aboriginal and Torres Strait Islander people in the workplace and to remove One's basic civil rights, reducing people subject to the Act to the position of state wards. It was intended to limit the reproduction of 'part-Aboriginal' offspring – the so-called 'half-caste menace' – seen at the time as a threat to an ideal 'White Australia'. In 1965 and 1971, new Protection Acts were passed that were also closely moulded on the original 1897 legislation.

Reflecting upon the creation of the British self-governing colony of Queensland in 1859 and the Federation of Australia on 1 January 1901, One realises that these beginnings do not arise out of universal principles of respect, equality and liberty for all. Neither are they founded on a common understanding, a signed Treaty between First Nations peoples and the Australian Nation, noble beliefs or shared values. They are built on, and as a result of, an egoic European mindset and culture of greed, judgement, separation and power over other people for political and personal gain.

Soon after the initial invasion by British forces and exploration of First Nations peoples' sovereign lands in various locations across Australia from 1788 onwards, life began to dramatically change for First Nations peoples. The first sign of these changes was the systematic acts of wilful sanctioned disbursement, destruction and denial of First Nations peoples' living existence. First Nations peoples fiercely resisted European occupation in many locations, which eventually gave rise to the colonial wars between First Nations and British troops, loyalists, squatters and settlers plus the addition of the indoctrinated and brutal reprisals of the native mounted police on Country.

While the motives of those opposing First Nations peoples may indeed be deeply questioned, the attempt to undertake the organised murder, killing and genocide of First Nations peoples is well documented. It is important to note that denying, erasing and ignoring real events in history is just one of the many tools used by colonising forces. It helps the 'colonisers' to idealise, rewrite and support the idea that the colonising values are better than those they are fighting against or intentionally oppressing. This is why the 'real' and 'actual' events of the British occupation of First Nations are not accurately taught in Australian schools even today. Although this part of Australian history is not considered a politically correct topic at the dinner table or in most modern conversations, it is a reality that reminds us all that Australia, like many other 'modern or reconstituted countries' in the world, arose out of collective egoic minds with a bloody thirst for conflict, senseless violence and a ruthless quest for power and possession of resources that belonged to First Nations.

It is significant to remember that no First Nations peoples formally surrendered independence on Country or conceded sovereignty after the colonial wars had ended, including the Butchulla (*Badtjala*) First Nation. The impact of perpetrated violence, together with the loss of access to natural resources, human and native title rights, and personal freedoms plus the transmission of infectious diseases and viruses all took their toll on First Nations families, children, young people, Elders, culture and the fabric of First Nations society. Life had significantly shifted for First Nations from independently living and existing in a thriving culture to simply surviving in a post-war colonialist culture of brutal greed, formal separation, structured oppression, social injustice and economic disempowerment. The impact of this organised, legalised and systematic governance of First Nations peoples has continued as a legitimate social policy and covert strategy for more than 200 years in Australia. It is now in its latest iteration, using more subtle strategies of digital disbursement, economic dependency and democratic denial.

The journey of intergenerational wellness, individual wellbeing and living in harmony on Country continues for most First Nations peoples today.

One is very grateful that One's parents were instrumental in mitigating the negative impacts of Queensland's various oppressive Acts upon One's family. This was achieved through strengthening One's access to higher education and increased economic opportunities, as well as social and cultural resilience. It was further assisted by acquiring stable housing, nurturing family wellbeing and strategically investing in One's family's future prosperity by moving to Sydney, New South Wales, in the mid 1970s.

On a brighter note, One's family was generally a harmonious loving space and consisted of mum and dad plus us kids – two girls and two boys. Being the eldest son had its own unique set of dutiful tasks, responsibilities and parental/family expectations. In order, there was One's older sister – Fiona, then Shawn (oneself), Mellissa and Rowan. A pretty 'normal nuclear family' living in the suburbs of Sydney, negotiating the dynamics of everyday family life. However, it was significantly different from most other families at the time because of One's parent's interracial marriage, shared values, aspirations, interests and virtues that were held within the family. One's family had many memorable annual family holidays on the traditional Country (land, sea and sky) of One's ancestors – the Butchulla (*Badtjala*) First Nation, visiting and staying on K'gari (Fraser Island) in Queensland for periods of up to a month or more in any one single year. This living adventure and other connections growing up provided One with cultural immersion in local Aboriginal stories, lore, beliefs, traditions, cultural practices and imprinted behaviours, which provided a strong emphasis on spirit and spiritual presence of oneself on Country and One's relationship to other spiritual Beings. It is through these and other experiences that One developed a great love and respect for Country, especially K'gari (Fraser Island).

One always considered the importance and relevance of these experiences as an important source of One's spiritual learnings, personal self-growth and positive wellbeing.

Like most people, One has experienced a range of diverse experiences throughout One's life to this present day. Some incredibly rewarding, some wonderfully uplifting and some inspiringly spiritual. Then on other occasions, some experiences would challenge the centrepoint of One's existing personhood, identity and beliefs. Whatever the moment, there has been one constant theme infusing and flowing throughout all of this lifestream of activities, events and happenings – One's inner knowing of things. Call it intuition, a gut feeling, a hint of being on track and in harmony to answering fundamental spiritual questions. A joining of all the dots or an alignment of mind–body–spirit together with a realisation of One's infinite existence or oneness with the universe itself. One sensed and felt it daily, and One continues to experience it now.

It is the same sort of feeling One gets when One notices oneself taking a relaxing deep breath on a cloudless day or how fresh water flows freely over One's body without resistance. It is an inner sense of eternal calm that silently dwells and is deeply present within One. As One travels through life, this inner contentment of One's spirit moves with One too.

As time and life naturally unfolded in One's life, a change also began to occur within One and to One's personhood and constructed identity. A quiet stillness and contented calmness began to be more and more present within oneself. It was a soothing reassuring feeling like the rustling sounds of the wind as it moved through the gum trees near One's coastal home in Hervey Bay, Queensland.

There's a lot to be said for those flashes of spiritual knowing that One experiences in life and how it gently calls to One's most inner Being. It is a quiet whisper that speaks to One in soft tones, saying things like, look this way, think this way, walk this way, or be aware of something or someone is coming. It is as familiar as One's mother's voice calling to One to come home or get inside now. One's spiritual awareness has always been drawn to this inner voice for change and to awaken.

One has been inspired by the following quote from the movie *Dune*, a 1984 American epic science fiction film written and directed by David Lynch, based on the 1965 Frank Herbert novel of the same name. In the scene, Jürgen Prochnow as Duke Leto Atreides is speaking with his son, Paul Atreides played by actor Kyle MacLachlan just prior to leaving One's homeworld of Caladan to travel across the universe to planet Arrakis (Dune). The Duke says:

> A person needs new experiences, they draw something deep inside allowing them to grow. Without change, some things sleep inside us and some things awaken. The sleeper must awaken.

These words express with great simplicity the idea that experiencing external change is integral to the awakening process. This is true for all Beings with a human form. This also includes people who currently have a particular spiritual practice, habit or participate in a spiritual-based religious culture and/or collective therapeutic gatherings.

The release of this movie in Australia coincided with the time One was just finishing One's studies in maritime electronics in Launceston, Tasmania, stepping into the world of work and expanding One's adult experiences and understanding of the world. The movie was a great catalyst for One to explore One's own known universe and make sense of it all. In a very real sense, it was its own spice that One needed to nudge One's consciousness in an expansive way.

The important point here is that the absence of change or challenges in One's life does not facilitate personal growth or spiritual awakening. There is no escape from One's way in the universe, not today, not tomorrow – not ever. While some may react in a negative way to this idea, look upon it as a blessing that the universe is on One's side to support One's higher self for One's greater good in life. Surrender to the silence of One's inner presence within the universe.

It is in this silence that One's inner voice of spirit will speak to One's mind–body to look this way, walk this way and be this way. Be aware of all that is in this moment of significance for oneself. In stillness, One can hear One's inner truth and it speaks to One in a language that is unbounded by time, space or belief.

Even during One's first serious partnership, spirit was speaking to One, whispering to One in a soft reassuring voice, but nevertheless always present. Spirit was a silent witness to One's life and life journey. No matter how difficult the experiences were at the time, Spirit was there, through the times of One's own increase in suffering in response to One's partner's mental health issues, the joy and stress of becoming a father for the very first time with the beautiful birth of One's eldest daughter, Narawi, the dismantling of One's significant investment in the design and development of an Indigenous not-for-profit community organisation and eco-cultural business, the breakup of One's personal partnership and the breakdown of One's family relationships, followed shortly after by the death of One's beloved mother (Shirley Foley nee Wondunna).

At this stage, One was feeling incredibly overwhelmed and experiencing some mental health issues of One's own. By the time the dust had settled, One was living out of town, back on One's half-acre rural property in a cosy and comfortable self-contained rural dwelling (a repurposed tin shed). One recognised that One desperately needed to slow right down, detach, decompress and develop some space for One to take some quality time to recover, reassess and recommit oneself to One's own wellness, personal mental health, positive wellbeing and a new lifestyle. A lifestyle that was free from dysfunctional relationships and extreme challenges.

Eventually, after some positive self-care, personal mental health maintenance and self-love, things got back on track. One began to re-engage with the world and rekindle One's relationship with One's daughter. One was in a better mind-body space because of these experiences and also knew that One was more resilient, experienced and familiar with some of life's complex adversities. One's gentleness was and will always be One's strength. One used this inner belief to reconfigure One's life – from the inside out. In moving forward with One's new life, One was aware that the universe would guide One on a totally different journey now. One's mind mistakenly thought that One had already learned all of One's important life lessons, and it could not possibly get any tougher or more challenging for One – but One's mind got it totally wrong. The universe had other plans for One, involving creating new and interesting situations for One's greater good and self-awakening. Time passed and One began the nurturing process of becoming whole once again and transforming One's life into a better space and place from which to re-engage with people and the world with renewed positivity and joyful enthusiasm.

Later on in life, One ventured into a new situation, relationship and marriage, raising a blended family with all of its mixed challenges and social complexities. During this time, One was somewhat distracted from One's own personal inner journey of awakening. However, as a parental caregiver to three First Nations children, including One's second daughter, Tulara, One found oneself returning again and again to many spiritual texts, books and artworks and synthesising the essence of these messages. Applying this spiritual information in One's daily life, relationships and at work was undertaken on an ad hoc basis with varying degrees of mindful and spiritual centredness. Mostly the result was a positive outcome for One and all. Even in the most challenging periods of personal disruption to One's life, One found that One's spirit was the

One and only constant in the universe that One could truly rely upon. One could consistently be with spirit in times when One's mind–body's was in need of great care, comfort and kindness. But One knew there was more ... more change to come and more to let go of and more to surrender of One's constructed personhood and from One's personal living space.

It was not until the passing away of the family German shepherd dog and burying him in the backyard, One's eldest teenage daughter's ego-centric pathway of individual identity defiance, the dissolving of One's seven-year marriage, the sale of One's amazing self-designed three-level family home and accumulated assets, the closure of One's cultural and community development consultancy business, and finally the death of One's father some five years later that One began another significant point of transformation and transcendence. At this moment, One was able to begin the process of finally surrendering and reconfiguring all the pieces of One's previous life into a greater sense of universal coherent awareness. One realised and awakened to a way that provided profound clarity, universal balance and harmony within a spiritual centredness. It was at this point that One felt a deep mental calm and inner spiritual peace. It was from this space that One knew that everything was going to be okay! One had been at this point of dramatic change in One's life before and One was once again at ease with One's eternal spiritual consciousness, spirit, soul and whole self.

But something had changed within, an unshakable knowingness in One's capacity to be and experience One's existence with a new awakened realisation. The realisation of the oneness within oneself and One with all.

A great profound calmness and serenity imbued One's sense of Being. Also, a feeling of lightness and joy too, as if a great weight had been lifted from One's personal responsibility and social obligations. It felt like One could finally breathe easy and effortlessly – freedom was One's oxygen and One needed this more than ever at this time. There was a subtle sweetness in the air now. Somehow it smelt like the morning scent of jasmine flowers or flowering blossoms from a gum tree. It was refreshing and could almost carry One away on the breeze if One chose to close One's eyes and imagine it.

What lay before One was a familiar and yet unknown path. One began to slowly reshape and reconstruct the pieces of One's life and at the same time move towards a turning point of spiritual singularity. One had co-created the 'right conditions' to manifest a significantly shifted awareness that surpassed all other moments that One had previously had on the planet. It didn't matter whether One was sitting at the beach enjoying the view of the ocean or at home relaxing in the backyard with the plants and birds or even walking along the Urangan Pier late at night with all the stars shinning in divine radiance and celestial splendour. The same inner sense of knowingness was always with One – One knew everything was going to be okay. There was something familiar about this moment – like One had been here many times before and yet it felt like the first time again – deja vu. One was comfortable continuing this journey, however now, One was is in an awakened state of infinite awareness of where One is.

The centrepoint of living had shifted for oneself, from where 'you are' to where 'One is'. This is important to remember, so let me say that again: the centrepoint of One's perception and living had realigned from 'You' or 'I' to within 'One'. That is, One has consciously chosen to realign One's sense of centre from being mind-centred to spirit-centred.

One's truth of knowingness had shifted; it was like changing One's fundamental knowledge platform or downloading a new app on One's smartphone. One could also think of it as shifting One's thoughts about the Earth being at the centre of the universe to now orbiting around the sun in a solar system within a galaxy, in a blink of an eye. One's mind was not now the centrepoint of One's life; it had shifted to the centredness of One's spiritual existence, enabling an awakened living experience. There was no turning point, no U-turn, no bridge to cross – it had been burned down or washed away in the flood of reformation, reconfiguration and realisation. There was only one way to go and that way was neither the 'old way' nor the 'new way' but 'the way' of One's self-realisation.

So now, One's internal compass did not point to the 'true north' of One's mind, but to the 'true truth' of One's spirit. An internal conscious shift had occurred from a 'you' view of living and belonging to a 'One' existence of being. One was free to be in life, be with life and be part of living an awakened life. Doing all the contemporary things that One usually does as part of the process of staying alive – exercising, going to work, cooking and cleaning, eating out, paying bills, attending meetings, being with friends and family, going on holidays, etc. But now One was engaging in these activities with a profoundly awakened sense of inner awareness and spiritual presence with oneself and all other sentient Beings.

Never doubt the value of experiencing personal challenges that enable profound changes within oneself.

This book is in essence a practical guide for making these changes at a very personal level to One's own life and living an awakened existence here and now on planet Earth. Also, think of it as a spiritual roadmap to life, the universe and everything. It points 'the way' toward One's own inner truth. A profound and deeply knowing place where One is and needs to be in One's life. It is about practical ways to create a spiritually centred life through mindful thinking and inspired living. Create the space and make the time to purposely and intentionally engage with One's life from a place of One's inner truth. This is the same truth that everyone knows deep down inside, and which is at the core of every human being on Earth. This fundamental and universal truth is: *Everything is Connected, All is One.*

Know that within One, One's spirit, soul or spiritual consciousness exists as an infusion of all of One's seven states of consciousness, including knowing, awareness, oneness, joy, free will, peace, and presence. These will be discussed in greater depth in later chapters of the book.

This book is a reflection on One's mind–body to consider the possibilities of change, transformation and transcendence. A renewal of One's inner spiritual truth in this world. With so many things going on in life and around the globe at the moment it is time for a meme (a thought) that cuts through the age-old pillars of poisoned political correctness, rises above the boundaries of selfish separateness and unifies the divisions of distinct identities and differences.

One is not here to conform to civil corruption or to band together in actions of opposing conflict. All those functions have only one purpose in common, to feed an egoic mind with an insatiable appetite for a self-serving agenda. One is strongly encouraged to not be part of the collective hoard of egoism and selfish separateness. Rise above this trivial temptation; embrace a universal way to live an inspired prosperous, abundant and awakened life.

One is invited to open One's mind, free One's spirit and live with a mindful awareness that is so profound that it will become one of the most significant turning points in One's life.

With transcendence, One's mind rises above, and with ascension, One's spirit awakens to the truth.

As One steps away from the 'you' identity or personhood that One has constructed and experienced, One will move towards the oneness of One's spirit. The 'you' identity in One's mind will encounter fierce and great resistance within oneself to let go. One's mind's ego will challenge 'you'. It will challenge any and all thoughts that arise to dissolve the illusion of its importance, identity and imagined reality. Reading this book may on occasion bring One into moments of uncomfortableness, with accompanying thoughts and feelings arising in One's mind–body that may seem in conflict with One's mind's current understanding of the world in which the 'you' identity lives. Let these thoughts and feelings arise, notice One's mind–body reaction as it happens, be in quiet observation as One is present within One's spirit and allow these hollow fears to fade away into the emptiness of no mind. Thoughts are like clouds on a windy day, they never stick around for long.

The spiritual nature of this book is about allowing One's mind's egoic complexities to be deconstructed and dissolved into the nothingness from which it was sourced.

Take a moment to enjoy the journey. Enjoy a quiet pause to fully appreciate a new way of looking at oneself and the universe. Allow the resonance of the words on these pages to permeate One's whole Being. Do not be surprised if they echo within One's inner-self and touch One in the deepest of ways that speak to One's innermost spiritual presence.

Throughout the book, One has applied and infused it with spiritual centredness and unconditional positivity, which has been a practice One has embraced throughout One's entire life. Even though we may never have met before, One has total belief in the person reading this book now. One also believes in One's ability, as the reader, to affect positive and everlasting changes in One's mind–body simply through thoughts, words and actions. Basically, people enable themselves to be One's own positive change agents by initiating actions to refresh, reconfigure and cultivate new thoughts, healthy habits and prosperous patterns, manifesting One's own destiny by transforming One's life, One's lifestyle and the world in which One lives now.

One believes that everyone exists within a state of infinite awareness within One's spiritual consciousness. In addition, when One aligns to this awareness, One is able to change One's current perspective. Through One's own awareness, One is able to change One's mind and, in doing so, change One's perspective. After all – perspective changes everything.

To change the thing that One is looking at, One simply needs to change the way that One is looking at it.

Living and shaping One's spiritual journey thus far has been about moving through a range of evolving human experiences and emotions (thoughts and feelings), particularly from the idea of finding 'your way' in the world to awakening to where

'One is' now. It is with endless gratitude that One affirms a great sense of thankfulness for all the sentient Beings One has had the pleasure of sharing One's life journey with on this planet.

It is with a deep and everlasting inner peace, as well as eternal calmness, that One has co-created this opportunity to share this information with One. The aim is to benefit others so that they are able to awaken oneself to One's inner spirit and invoke infinite joy within oneself. A gift from a single Being to another, here and now.

This book is structured in seven chapters. Each chapter focuses on a specific spiritual topic of interest and contains quotes from well-known, international spiritual speakers, thought leaders and mindfulness Masters that further highlight and emphasise the key concepts in the chapter. This adds to ease of understanding and assists One to gain a greater appreciation of the issues, ideas and concepts being discussed. During the writing process, some key issues have been explored at length, as this has been necessary for reasons of clarification. One may find it necessary to re-read and review some sections and quotes several times in order to understand them at a deeper and more profound level.

Some of the ideas, concepts and suggestions explored may significantly challenge One's current perspective of One's personhood or individual identity. One may need to create some space and quiet time in One's life to reflect on One's overall mindset or mindscape. This will most likely include some self-analysis of One's current residual self-image or personhood, identity, world view and universal order – including One's existence within the universe. One may have a strong mind–body reaction to these suggestions. One may want to nurture key issues, ideas and concepts and then revisit them at a later date – that's okay too! Take time to review and reflect without judgement, prejudice or attachment. Simply be open and allow One's spirit to guide One as One's mind–body–spirit considers these ideas and suggestions – after all, a thought is just a thought and it can be changed at any moment, should One's mind choose to do so.

When reading this book, One is free to begin wherever One feels most comfortable. One may find that One's mind–body experiences heightened levels of excitement or a 'spiritual high' when engaging in the book or when One's mind–body attains an 'A-ha, One's mind gets it' moment. Some may be ready for this experience; however, for others it may be delayed and require some additional processing or comfort time and space. Simply accept that the right space and place for One's understanding is also at One's own pace. All things happen in the right moment wherever One is.

A range of diverse and interrelated key topics are discussed in this book, including spirit, knowing, the way, relationships, change, conscious choice and inspiration. At the end of every chapter is a section called 'Living One's Inner Way Now', which summarises suggestions to help One put all the learnings, teachings, and pointings into practice within One's daily life.

This book acts like a 'walk-with' person, providing spiritual companionship as One walks each other 'home' along a path of One's inner truth. One knows and believes that One already holds the key to self-realisation and self-enlightenment within One. It is just a matter of realising what already is … then staying centred in this infinite beingness within oneself.

Relax, take a deep breath … and let's begin this exciting joyful journey together now.

ONE EXISTS, SO ONE IS.

CHAPTER 1

Spirit
Divinity Within One

Spirit as One

The first and most basic truth of the universe is to realise that One is and will always be an eternal, immortal and infinite spirit.

Everything in the universe begins and ends with spirit, soul or cosmic consciousness. Spirit can also be referred to as creative source consciousness or Source Consciousness, also known simply as the Source, God, Allah, the Great Creator, Krishna consciousness or divine pure consciousness, whichever One feels more comfortable when thinking about One's inner spirit while reading this book.

As a spiritual entity or spirit, the essential message of truth that flows throughout this entire book is: *Spirit is One – One is Spirit.* The terms 'One' and 'spirit' are easily interchangeable, and may assist the reader in distinguishing a spiritual perspective where the term 'One' primarily refers to One's spirit. This is an important and key concept to understand as One moves deeper into a greater appreciation of spirit and how it relates to oneself and One's life.

In understanding One's journey here on Earth, One must begin by realising who and what One is now. Know that as spirit, One exists in the universe as a nameless, formless, ageless, sexless, genderless, dimensionless, shapeless, weightless, unchanging divine entity free of any atomic particles or waves and without mind or body. Spirit is not something that One can specifically point to in the universe, although it is ever present in One's life. One cannot capture, contain, control, corrupt, cure or kill it in any way, even though it exists within One at this very moment. As a spirit, One is and will never be alive and hence will never die. Life and death are only a distinction created in One's mind to explain the manifesting shifts in lifeforms during the living process and beyond the dying process. One's journey through the universe is a spiritual relationship within an infinite continuum of being, moving from pure consciousness to hosting a manifested form (e.g. human or animal) or altered consciousness and then back to One's original state of pure consciousness.

One is integral to the oneness of the divine order within the universe. As part of this divine chaos, One flows effortlessly within an infinite continuum of beingness.

One can never run away from One's inner spirit no matter how hard One may try and hide from this truth. Buddha says:

> Three things cannot long be hidden, the sun, the moon and the truth.

It is impossible to delete, destroy or dismiss the divine essence from One's inner Being – this truth is undeniable. One is unable to change or swap One's spirit for another person's spirit. There is no replacement, upgrade or renewal of One's spirit. What One is within, is within One now and forevermore.

One's existence as a spirit is integral to One's infinite beingness within pure consciousness. No individual person on Earth or in the universe can escape the divine Being that exists within One now. One cannot remove spirit from the human mind–body, although One's spirit may will itself to leave and go back to the Source and not host One's human form any longer, due to a range of reasons such as terminal illness or disease, fatal accident or assault, self-harm, death by misadventure or another critical disaster or life-terminating injury.

The important thing to remember is that spirit can never ever be hurt, harmed or injured by any human beliefs, thoughts, actions or behaviours. This is a fundamental spiritual principle of existence and occurs throughout One's entire life while being present on Earth or in space or anywhere else in the solar system or the universe. From the time One's mind–body is born right through to the time One's mind–body dies, it is only One's mind's identification with One's ego that leads to self-inflicted pain and suffering in One's mortal life. Spirit exists beyond all acts of hatred, violence and unkindness in the world. It does not matter who One is (male, female or other sexual identities) or One's family, culture, tribe, clan, band, language group, traditional country, society, First Nation, nation-state or nationality. Spirit as pure consciousness is without judgement, attachment or resistance to any and all acts of inhumanity committed by human beings upon each other.

Think of it this way: One's mind–body may be subject to all the sensations and experiences of being human. However, One's spirit exists within a continuum of infinite beingness and as such is not bound by time, space, human laws, or One's living experiences while One is host to a human form. Spirit is a silent witness and divine observer of One's mind–body's thoughts, feelings, beliefs, behaviours, actions and life.

The simplest way to think about being a single divine entity within a cosmic collective of divine Beings is to imagine One's spirit as the wave of an infinite ocean. As the wave is the ocean, so too One's spirit is the Source of consciousness or infinite oneness itself. Every single wave upon the surface of the ocean contains within it the pure essence of the ocean. The divinity of the wave and ocean exist as One. What is within the wave also exists within the ocean – they are the same, only perceived in a different way.

Know that One is not a human being having a spiritual experience, One is a spiritual Being hosting the experience of One's human form. When One is present on Earth, One is host to whatever form of human (male or female, including all sexual identities) One has chosen and the experiences of this manifestation. This is an important point to pay particular attention to in One's life. Most people believe that, as a human being, experiencing One's spirit is an optional extra, like downloading a new app on One's smartphone. One appears to have the option to choose to use it or not. Spirit does not and will never work like this in One's life. One needs to appreciate that spirit always comes first when it chooses to be present on Earth. Spirit as a divine entity is host to One's human or animal form. This is the way it has been since the beginning or existence of Source Consciousness.

In knowing spirit at a deep, personal and more intimate level, One must first be aware of the seven truths about One which are the beginning point for One's spiritual journey here on Earth.

The seven truths of 'One' or Spirit are:

1. One is, and will always be, an eternal, immortal and infinite spiritual Being.
2. One is a free spirit, existing in an endless continuum of infinite beingness beyond space and time (non-dimensional, multi-state-based existence).
3. One is oneness, nameless, formless, timeless, shapeless, sexless, egoless, fearless, selfless and pure cosmic consciousness itself.
4. One exists in any or all of the seven states of divine consciousness (knowing, awareness, oneness, joy, free

will, peace and presence) at any given moment in the universe.
5. One is spirit, soul or cosmic consciousness and host to One's human (mind–body) form and manifested experiences in the universe.
6. One co-exists in a divine synergy of pure consciousness (spirit) and altered consciousness (mind–body).
7. One is here now to awaken to One's spiritual reality and be present in this moment as a sentient Being of the universe to exist, express and experience conscious mindful living and being now as part of One's journey of infinite existence.

In understanding these seven truths, One must also be aware of what is not true about One. It is important to know that:

- One is not One's mind or any thought that has or will ever be created within it.
- One is not One's body, regardless of its shape, colour, ethnicity, race, size, age, height, weight, gender, appearance by virtue of its DNA code or how it is clothed, modified or presented to the world in which One lives.
- One is not One's partnership/parenting/family/sibling/kinship role or relationship, even though it may have been and continue to be integral to One's socio-economic-cultural development, eco-enviro conditioning, moral/ethical shaping and engagement on a daily basis.
- One is not One's place or position in society, even if One has been elevated to it through natural birth, personal achievement or specific circumstances, chance, luck, longevity, deeds, fame, celebrity status, popularity, election, social pursuits, acknowledgements or group accolades.
- One is not One's achievements, even if One has spent a lifetime working with people to create a positive change

or improve the world One lives in through simple acts of care, kindness and compassion or through life-changing inventions, making incredible discoveries, doing ground-breaking research or inspiring new innovations.
- One is without religion, belief, ideology, gender, sexuality, race, culture, age or nationality.
- One is without concern, worry, anxiety, disease, illness or fear.
- One is without attachment, resistance or judgement of any and all things in the universe too.

If One is none of these things associated with human activity or One's human form, One may very well ask the question – who is One?

One's inner spirit

The first step in knowing One or One's spirit is to be aware of One's infinite existence. This is key to bringing spiritual awareness into One's life and living life from a spirit-centred perspective. When One is living One's life in this way, One aligns One's mind–body–spirit together as a united Being of love and light in this world – here and now.

Be aware that One is of the same oneness which exists in everybody on Earth. Every sentient Being that has ever lived on this beautiful planet is One. All is One in the universe too, but this topic will be explored in greater detail in a later chapter. Every spiritual Being is of the exact sameness or oneness as everyone else – there is only the same oneness within each and all of humanity. The only thing that distinguishes One from another Being is the specific configuration of One's mind–body thoughts, form and the expression of this mind–body within the bound relativities of space and time. All who appear in front of One throughout One's entire life journey are part of the great illusion which is manifested out of altered consciousness. Everybody who appears in human form will eventually be naturally deconstructed into individual random molecules, atoms, particles, waves and energy once again. All human forms will be reused, repurposed and recycled – the universe wastes nothing.

The human form in all its diversity around the world is only an image of manifested altered consciousness which is hosted by One's spirit. It is a temporary manifestation without any permanence in life. A shadow on the mist of time in an ever-changing landscape. Everyone is just a spiritual visitor to Earth on a temporary divine visa within the universe.

One is the host to One's mind–body, however most people think that One's mind–body is the host for One's spirit – this is where a lot of people become confused and have it back to front. A human being is in essence a synergy of altered consciousness (mind–body) within pure consciousness (One or spirit).

Another example that illustrates this idea is when a mother is pregnant and about to give birth to a baby. If One considers for a moment after the spirit of the baby has arrived within the mother's womb and is already spiritually aligned with the baby. What exists now is altered consciousness (baby's mind–body) within pure consciousness (One or spirit of the baby). This configuration is now also within altered consciousness (mother's mind–body) within pure consciousness (One or spirit of the mother), so on and so forth. The mother then lives in altered consciousness (the material/physical world) within pure consciousness (Oneness of the universe). This is how the universe works, both moving inwards and moving outwards. This can all seem a bit confusing at first, but it is really a simple idea to grasp. Know that all altered consciousness and pure consciousness co-exist with each other and provide a natural point of equilibrium, balance and harmony.

One is able to transcend altered consciousness that is the material or physical world by being in a free will state of consciousness. This is because One exists within a dimensionless state or infinite beingness, so One is able to pass through the material or physical world as it has no effect on One's spirit at all. This happens every time a person passes away and when One's spirit leaves One's human form and returns to Source or non-dimensional consciousness field.

However, One or spirit has the inherent capacity to inter-dimensionally align with its own altered state of consciousness – this is One of the prime principles for the existence of life, the universe and everything. This is how One aligns perfectly with One's mind–body inside One's mother's womb. There is no slippage or misalignment when a state of divine synergy exists between One's altered consciousness (mind–body) and pure consciousness (One or spirit). It is the basis upon which all else is manifested.

In coming to a place of inner knowing about One's spirit and its origins, lets now accept for a moment, without resistance or reservation, that pure consciousness is the One and only point of spiritual singularity or Source of all things in the universe. In the beginning, within this spiritual singularity through the Oneness of divine free will, pure consciousness created altered consciousness. A way for pure consciousness to experience itself. Now this may seem quiet silly an idea at first. But, when One comes to think of it, it is like playing a simple game of hide and seek. Just like when One did when One was a child, nothing more – nothing less. The only difference is that it is taking place between the pure consciousness or God consciousness or the Creator and itself. This is the simplest and most profound truth for the existence of One and all things in the universe.

When One talks about altered consciousness, know that One is referring to the classic model of the known universe (e.g. matter – everything on Earth, energy – all forms, space, time, planets, solar systems, stars and galaxies).

Great sages, Masters, philosophers, wise men and Elders have all known this prime truth since time began as, *everything is connected – all is One.*

One's mind does not need proof to believe this prime truth in order for it to be true – spirit simply accepts what 'is' in the universe. The same principle applies to spirit, just because One cannot see One's spirit, does not mean that it doesn't exist. Everyone knows that One's spirit exists but are unable to proof it in a standard tangible or scientific way with empirical evidence. This is because it is impossible to prove something which exists in a dimensionless state of existence by the quantifiable rules and laws contained within a three dimensional world. Pure spiritual consciousness or spirit is beyond the quantum laws of physics and will never be able to be quantified or defined by any human law, theory or principle. There is no evidence in this tangible world that will prove to a non-believer that One is an intangible, dimensionless, formless divine entity existing within an infinite continuum of beingness.

Another way of thinking and looking at this situation is to think about the universe in terms of light and dark. Without light there is no darkness, without darkness there is no light – both need each other in order to co-exist. Otherwise everything would be in darkness or everything would be in light. This duality is necessary for infinite balance, harmony and the divine chaos in which the known universe manifests itself.

Now imagine for a moment that there are One hundred students all studying natural science or the environment. What if these One hundred students were all given a single young plant all from the same seed stock, in an identical container and were individually instructed to follow the same precise care and training without contact with the other students. The end result after a reasonable period of time would be that each student's plant would be the same genetically and yet different. Due to a range of interpretation variances such as water, light, care and nurturing by each student. This same principle can also be applied to One's mind–body development, journey of enlightenment or path along an awakening process.

The purpose of living life is to awaken within it. One may interpret, shape and configure infinite and interesting ways in which to live One's life, however One's spirit will remain unchanged – this is a constant in the universe.

Changing One's awareness

Dr Wayne Dyer, an American philosopher, self-help author and motivational speaker, says:

> When you change the way you look at things, then the things which you look at also changes.

This is true at both at a micro and macro level. It also occurs within every aspect of One's life, community, society, First Nation, nation state, the world and the universe.

As One deconstructs, dissolves and removes all the blockages of illusions from One's mind, One enables oneself to see the majestic beauty of One's divinity. There is no distance or space between oneself and One's divine spirit, only the illusion within One's own egoic mind distracting One from aligning with what already exists within One this present moment of now.

Marianne Williamson, an American spiritual teacher, author, lecturer, and activist says:

> Our deepest fear is not that we are inadequate. Our deepest fear is that we are powerful beyond measure. It is our light, not our darkness that most frightens us. We ask ourselves, 'Who am I to be brilliant, gorgeous, talented, fabulous?' Actually, who are you not to be? You are a child of God. Your playing small does not serve the world. There is nothing enlightened about shrinking so that other people won't feel insecure around you. We are all meant to shine, as children do. We were born to make manifest the glory of God that is within us. It's not just in some of us; it's in everyone. And as we let our own light shine, we unconsciously give other people permission to do the same. As we are liberated from our own fear, our presence automatically liberates others.

This quote from Marianne Williamson is a magnificent guide that is capable of inspiring One to shift One's self-perception to be a more divine and radiant Being of the universe. If One seeks to change One's life and living circumstances from despair to joy, poverty to prosperity, or darkness to light then it is necessary for One to alter One's awareness of oneself.

On occasions, One goes for a mindful early morning walk in the community where One lives. When One's mind–body is walking along the footpath, walkway or beach it is common practice to extend a friendly joyful greeting like, 'good morning', 'morning' or 'Gid-day' to other walkers. This simple greeting is how One gives thanks and shows One's gratitude for being alive and for all the beautiful things in One's life. One is so grateful for the fresh air that fills One's lungs, One's legs to carry One's body through the exercise process and the beauty of nature in all its diversity, colours and configurations. One is also grateful for the sun as it shines its early morning light through the leaves as it rises up behind the coastal gum trees and over the sea. Life is truly a divine gift and One is blessed with enjoying this life.

One sometimes wonders what other people are thinking at this time of day as they pass on bye. Do they perceive themselves as a divine Being of the universe or just a person with a body doing some exercise because it is good for One's health and wellbeing? Are people so caught up in One's mind's illusion that it is preventing One from seeing One's divinity within? Do people really fear the light within oneself so much that they prefer to hide in the darkness of shame and ignorance? Do people simply opt out of listening to One's spirit because One's mind perceives it to be too confronting or painful? Or, are people just so comfortable and familiar with living within the shadows of false truths of One's egoic mind that One's mind is now conditioned to this pattern of belief and behaviours on a daily basis? Whatever the reason, it is not until One looks inwards that One will find a new life outwards. Know that it is One's own ego and allowing it to construct and maintain the illusion which misinforms and manipulates One's living experiences away from being spirit centred. Only when One's perception of oneself is altered and One shifts from an 'I am' to 'One is' perspective then One will have transitioned to a different point of view. One will then be able to journey through life in a spirit centred way. Know that changing One's inner landscape requires courage, kindness and a commitment to be One now.

Many people are not comfortable or familiar with embracing One as a formless dimensionless spirit existing within an infinite continuum of beingness. The thought of this alternate perspective and divine reality goes against the vast majority of formal teachings, schooling and training which have been provided to One's mind-body since an early age. Countless generations of people all over the world have been systematically conditioned by the previous generation and One's peers through educational institutions to ignore, suppress and disregard spirit. Spirit and its place in One's daily life has not been acknowledged, validated or celebrated as an important part of One's life and yet it is integral to all things in the universe. The practice which embraces One, One's spirit or spiritual consciousness is the path to One's freedom, prosperity and abundance in this life.

When coming to answering the big questions of life, the universe and everything, such as 'Who am I?' Most people are unaware that this is not the right question for the answer that One seeks. The question that people need to ask is 'Who is One?' When the question is changed then so too will the answer be. Millions of people all over the world over identify oneself with One's mind and its thoughts, One's body and how it looks, One's position, language and culture, One's possessions and all the material things in One's life, One's relationship status, One's achievements and how much One earns, One's friends/family member's opinions and perspectives of oneself, etc. Know that One, as a spiritual Being, One will never be any of these things. One is the observer of any and all human conditions or conditioning – One is first, last and always free of human limitations.

As a divine Being of the universe, One's purpose is to be here now – fully awake, completely engaged and totally detached. This may seem like a contradiction, however, as One awakens so will One's life become more deeply engaged and at the same time One will be more peacefully detached from specific outcomes in One's life. Know that when One demands nothing of the world, nor of God/the Creator/the universe, when One wants nothing, seeks nothing, expects nothing, then a supreme state of infinite beingness will come to One uninvited and unexpected.

In changing One's awareness to be more spiritually centred, One will be able to access divine guidance in every moment of One's life on Earth. If One's mind–body is currently not in this space or place, then it is critical that One's egoic mind stops it's resistance to change and acts in the best interest of One's higher-self. This is the moment to accept that One's path will be found on the road which One tries to avoid it – so, it is best to be the change One seeks to be now.

Looking within Oneself

What if One simply accepted One's divinity as a spiritual being of the universe? How different would One's life be on Earth? One would realise that the planet is home to billions of visiting entities, each One would be host to a different human form, and all moving through the same process of experiencing One's humanness. There would be obvious shifts in the ways in which One would perceive and think about oneself and others in One's life. One would begin with an altered awareness of One's true identity as a spiritual Being within a continuum of beingness. One would realise that One is an integral part of the universe itself. This shift alone will have incredible positive effects within One's life, and ripple outwards to touch and influence One's friends, family, First Nation, tribe, band, community, society and nation. One would project an outward appearance of inner calm, mindful clarity and living confidence as One went about One's daily chores and tasks. One would not be particularly concerns about negative social media posts and personal conflicts in One's circles of interests, as it would distract One from One's own inner peace and personal wellbeing. One would not doubt One's capacity to do things because One would have no doubt that whatever One put One's mind to, it could be done. One would act with positive goodwill and in good faith with others whilst committing to a cooperative process of mutual benefit and at the same time letting go of the outcome.

When One looked into a mirror, One would not see a human being looking back at oneself. One would recognise the reflection of a divine Being powerful beyond measure. A Being with divine radiance to light One's own path and thus light a path for all others in this world too. One would be fully capable of attracting and manifesting all that One could imagine and desire in One's life. One's mind and body would be looked upon and treated with positive intent, nurturing it with care, kindness and compassion. One's mind would be seen as a divine space for creating thoughts which aligned to the oneness of the universe. One's physical presence in the universe would be viewed as a divine miracle. One would simply be in complete awe and wonder of all that One is now.

One's divine radiance is best encouraged and celebrated each and every day. Changing One's awareness raises the positive vibrational energy and spiritual alignment of all people on the planet. The more people who change One's inner awareness of One's spirit, the more it creates a critical mass of awakening for all of humanity. Eventually, in time it will reach a tipping point for all people on Earth. A new time will emerge where One will know that One is spirit, it will be common place knowledge. Like accepting and understanding that the world is not flat, but round, and that the earth is not the centre of the universe but orbits the sun within a solar system and galaxy. A paradigm shift will have occurred in all human minds as to who One is now. This will be the catalyst for a new global vision through One's awareness of spirit and all things divine in One's life.

Carl Jung, a Swiss psychiatrist and psychoanalyst who founded analytical psychology, says:

> Your vision will become clear only when you can look into your own heart. Who looks outside, dreams; who looks inside, awakes.

To change One's outside experiences of life, One must begin by changing One's internal mental landscape first. In order to live a spirit centred life One will need to change One's awareness within this present moment. This will require a change from One's mind centredness to spirit centredness. A shift from being driven by One's mind's ego to being inspired by One's spirit and intuitive alignment with the universe. The way to transform One's awareness is through a profound realisation of who One is now. It is important to know that change, growth and spiritual awakening will not occur in the absence of personal pain, suffering or challenges in One's life. Buddha taught that One suffers when One's mind clings to or resists experiences, especially when One's mind wants life to be different from what it is now. Buddha says:

> Pain is inevitable but suffering is optional.

When painful sensations arise in One's life, and if One meets these experiences with mindful clarity and One's spiritual presence, One will be able to see that pain is just pain without any emotion. When One is mindful of pain rather than reacting to it, One does not shrink into the experience of victimised self-suffering. One is truly capable of rising above all of One's suffering through One's mindfulness and spiritual presence.

Be the change One's mind seeks in One's life. It is important to remember that conscious change is not a passive action, it requires One to actively apply One's mind–body–spirit with mindful intention to change One's life and living experiences.

There are three things that One can do to change One's awareness to live a more spirit-centred life and lifestyle:

1. **Accept** all that is present now in this moment without attachment, judgement or resistance. Be aware that all things will happen as a function of the divine synchronicity of the universe. Each and every moment flowing and unfolding into the next moment as part of the perfect sequencing and timing of the universe. When the moment is right, it will be the right moment for One to experience.
2. **Allow** One's internal point of perception of One's spirit, oneself and One's place in the universe to completely change as One lets go of the illusion that has been constructed within One's egoic mind. Embrace a new way of looking at and perceiving One's life, living experiences and whole of life.
3. **Align** One's mind–body–spirit as One's true divine identity and presence on Earth now. Affirm with absolute certainty and positive conviction that One is powerful beyond measure, with the capacity to co-create or manifest any mindful intention that One seeks to experience in the universe. Be open to co-creating an inter-dimensional gateway between pure consciousness (One or One's spirit) and altered consciousness (mind–body) by being virtuous. Live in harmony and balance as One flows effortlessly without attachment, judgement or resistance in One's life.

Accepting all in this moment

Eckhart Tolle, a well-known contemporary spiritual teacher and modern day global influencer on spiritual thinking and living in the now, says:

> Accept – then act. Whatever the present moment contains, accept it as if you had chosen it. Always work with it, not against it. Make it your friend and ally, not your enemy. This will miraculously transform your whole life.

Know that all change begins with acceptance. This is achieved by letting go and aligning One's mind–body to the reality of what is now. Acceptance is about perceiving the current situation as it is and surrendering to this reality. This means looking at life not through distorted cultural lenses, brightly coloured glasses or sugar coating situations, events or activities. It simply means keeping things real, natural and free of personally biased thinking, conditional perceptions or self-moderating social filters. When One's mind is open and honest with oneself then this will be reflected in One's life. One will bring more clarity and knowingness as One journeys along One's spiritual path. Being truthful connects oneself to the universe. By doing this, One is able to check-in to One's inner spirit, speak from One's spiritual heart and centre oneself within One's spiritual consciousness. One must first sip from One's inner truth and only then will One know that this truth comes from the same pure waters of oneness that creates life and sustains One's existence in the universe.

Osho, also known as Acharya Rajneesh, an Indian godman, leader of the Rajneesh movement and mystic, says:

> Truth is not something outside to be discovered, it is something inside to be realised.

While every human being approaches life in various different ways, there are some aspirations that all of humanity share. Most humans aspire to attain a certain level of comfort in the world that is free of pain, fear and suffering. It is a perfectly natural human desire to seek to live a happy and meaningful life. The real question is not about 'what' One will do in life, but 'how' One will do it. By aligning One's mind and body to One's spirit, One is able to live a more peaceful, prosperous and, of course, contented life.

An inquiring mind is driven to seek answers to questions, whereas spirit already knows the realities of One's existence.

One is free to choose how One experiences One's human life, be it from centredness within mind–body to the exclusion of spirit or from within centredness of spiritual consciousness inclusiveness of mind–body. One is imbued with divine free will to choose whichever path One seeks to experience in this moment now.

One can either live an egoic mind-centred life or a divine spirit-centred life. These are the two most profound ways that One's human experiences are realised.

The first step in realising an awakened life is being aware of One's spiritual consciousness and the infinite beingness in which it exists. One is able to accept and affirm this inner truth through direct experience of One's spirit and its seven states of consciousness. In effect, what One ends up doing is shifting One's place of perspective to a state of perception. It is as if One's thinking has moved from an 'I am' place of belonging to 'One is' state of being.

One realises this act of surrender by letting go of everything and being the observer of oneself and One's mind–body. By doing this, One transcends One's original mind-centred perspective and aligns to an infinite state of spiritual awareness within One's spirit. Whatever the universe removes from One's life, just let it go.

To illustrate this point of shifted sense of perspective to perception further, let One retell a story that was shared by the spiritual teacher Mooji.

Imagine that there are two identical birds in a tree. One bird is a physical bird (tangible/visible) on the lower branch and One bird is a spiritual bird (intangible/invisible) on the branch above it. Let's assume that the physical bird is unaware of the spiritual bird watching it, but can somehow feel its presence there in the tree. The physical bird is busy building a nest on the lower branch while the other bird (the spirit of the physical bird) watches its ongoing activities and busyness in the tree as it flies back and forth to gather twigs, grasses and other material for the nest. Now, let's pretend for a moment to be the bird in the higher branch, noticing all the activities, thoughts, feelings and behaviours of the physical bird below. Be silent and still, noticing everything – simply look on without any reactive thoughts, feelings, emotions, attachment, resistance or judgement. Simply be present with unconditional acceptance, infinite peace and with joyful intentions for the physical bird. This is what spirit does in real life within One.

What ego does within One's mind is to convince oneself that One is only the physical bird or human form, but actually One's real presence in life and the universe is the spirit bird. Know that One is not the physical bird on the lower branch (altered consciousness manifesting as mind–body). One is the non-physical bird (spiritual consciousness) on the higher branch. However, both birds seamlessly co-exist within the same bird as a synchronous fusion of mind–body–spirit in the universe.

When One is in total acceptance of all that is and will be in the universe, One is in an awakened state of pure spiritual awareness. Buddha says:

> Awake. Be the witness of your thoughts. You are what observes, not what you observe.

Allowing everyone and everything to just be

When One allows everyone and everything to just be, One discovers that One is able to create quality spaces in One's life for mindful living and to be present in the moment. Mindful practice offers One's mind a way to let go. Through creating spaces in One's life, One is able to quieten the mind, soothe the body and simply be with One's spirit.

Know that the universe has no need to be in control of anything – it just is. The universe wants for no single thing or for any particular moment to be a certain way. It simply exists as altered consciousness within a field of infinite possibilities. All that is and will ever be, already exists in the universe in One form or another – now. Just because One is unable to see it or experience a certain thing does not mean that it doesn't exist. Everything occurs at the exact moment of its divine manifestation. Even stars and galaxies come into being when they are supposed to and then dissolve back into stardust when the time is right. All manifestations in nature and life happen in perfect order, sequence and harmony within the universe.

One cannot make a fruit tree blossom when it suits One, nor make it bear fruit before its time. Everything unfolds at exactly the right time it needs too. One will never fulfil One's own destiny in life until One's mind lets go of the illusion of control. To do this, One's mind needs to be still and open to the possibility that things are the way they are because of the way things are in life. Lao Tzu (also known as Laozi), an ancient Chinese philosopher and writer, reputed author of the *Tao Te Ching*, founder of philosophical Taoism and a deity in religious Taoism and traditional Chinese religions, says:

> To a mind that is still, the whole universe surrenders.

As rain falls effortlessly from the sky, rivers flow naturally to the ocean and sun shines during the day, so do the stars come out at night. All is in perfect balance and harmony in the universe. There is nothing that needs to be added or taken away from it. It is the way of all things and all things flow in this way. It is the universe being itself – complete truth and beauty from the same oneness.

Simply by allowing things to be as they are, One is able to see the true beauty of nature and life as it effortlessly unfolds around One. Do nothing and the tide still comes in. Lao Tzu also says:

> By letting go, it all gets done.

One knows with absolute certainty that nature and everything that is manifested within it is an expression of pure divine natural wonder and magnificence. With One's eyes closed shut and One's mind wide open, One is able to truly see the brilliant unending radiance of an abundant universe.

When One is knowingly true to One's inner spirit, the universe will naturally guide and support One's life and positive living experiences. Do not be distracted by the day-to-day necessities or social conformities of modern life. Stop trying to be somewhere or someone else. Just be joyful being One, with whatever is in One's life. Create quality spaces to give One's mind and body a break from thinking about being somewhere else in life. Pause and reflect for a moment. Sit and be still. Gently take a series of long deep breaths. Then say to oneself, in this quiet and silent moment, that 'it's okay', 'everything is going to be okay', and 'the universe is on One's side'. It is perfectly okay for One to be where One is now. This is the perfect place for One to be while continuing One's spiritual journey on Earth and on One's path of awakening. Everything is going to be okay in the end. Acknowledge that One lives in an abundant universe and on an amazing planet – Earth. One is here now. One is blessed and grateful to be in this space at this exact moment in time. So be and live here – now. Create and make living this moment, a moment for living One's life to the best of One's abilities. Consider that every breath is a gift of life, and every heartbeat within One's body is in rhythmic harmony with the universe. One's optimum life and living experiences will only be experienced in true alignment with the natural order of the universe. Breathe, live and flow with the divine rhythm of the universe. Wherever One is – this is home.

Aligning One's vibration with One's spirit and the universe

When One looks at a rainbow, One is witnessing the divine light of the universe. When One is spiritually aligned with One's pure consciousness, One is experiencing the divinity of the universe within oneself.

Humans have observed rainbows since the dawn of humanity. There are many myths, superstitions and cultural interpretations about the rainbow and rainbow spirit and what it means to people within various cultures around the world. Many First Nations peoples believe that it is a sign from the creator, supreme spiritual Being or some special divine or dreamtime message for those who are witnessing its manifestation. Around 350BCE the Greek philosopher Aristotle began his thoughtful reflections about rainbows and their colours. In about 5CE, the Roman philosopher Seneca the Younger, in the first book of his *Naturales Quaestiones* series, noted Aristotle's ideas and elaborated upon them. Surprisingly, Seneca was ahead of his time in reasoning about such things, which led him to predict the prism effect many centuries before Isaac Newton.

Over time, there have been many philosophers, thinkers and naturalists who have examined the phenomenon of the rainbow effect in the sky and during other circumstances. However, limited consideration has been given to exploring the idea that the rainbow effect may also exist in a non-dimensional realm and apply to One's spirit or non-dimensional state of consciousness.

Isaac Newton proved that white light is made up of a spectrum of colours by splitting light with a prism of glass. When this is done, One is able to clearly view the bands of individual colours across the entire spectrum, which together form white light. Newton's work, along with the work of others before him, showed conclusively how rainbows are formed in the sky and life. It was also noted that the sequence of colours never changes along the spectrum: red, orange, yellow, green, blue, indigo and violet.

Even today, the idea of seven colours of the rainbow persists in society and is very obvious to the naked eye when the sun is shining brightly after a rain shower. Upon closer scientific inspection, One can see that there are far more than just seven individual hues that form the rainbow.

One's divine spirit is imbued with the same rainbow effect as white light and has seven states of spiritual consciousness. As One can see the individual wavelengths that flow in perfect harmony to form white light, One can also experience all seven states of divine consciousness. These states of consciousness are Knowing – Awareness – Oneness – Free will – Peace – Joy – Presence. All these states of consciousness originate within One. Know that there is no distance or space between oneself and One's divine states of consciousness. One can experience a single, multiple or all states of consciousness at any moment in the universe.

Across the ages and through the many learnings, teachings and pointings of great thinkers, philosophers, teachers, Masters, gurus and direct personal experiences, One is aware that there is a relationship that exists between One's states of consciousness and One's virtues. No scientific papers have been published, that One is aware of, in this area of interest. It is a field of human study that, by its very nature, is at the intersection of dimensional and non-dimensional existence. However, there is a divine correlation between specific states of consciousness and particular virtues within One's mind–body–spirit.

Even if One is in the process of transcendence and ascension of One's higher-self or consciousness, One is able to create virtuous habits and a centred life practice for daily living. If nothing else, it simply makes good sense to live virtuously. Being virtuous creates the opportunity to align oneself to the infinite beingness within which spiritual consciousness exists.

One knows that every spiritual state of consciousness has a corresponding virtue as part of altered consciousness, what One refers to as the rainbow effect or rainbow principle of inter-dimensional alignment. These are:

Spiritual State – Virtue
Knowing – Compassion
Awareness – Helpfulness
Oneness – Acceptance
Free will – Simplicity
Peace – Patience
Joy – Generosity
Presence – Openness

Through embracing the seven virtues detailed above, One is able to align One's mind–body to the infinite beingness of One's existence by 'being' virtuous. There is a natural synergy of alignment between One's virtues and states of consciousness. When One is in this phased alignment, One experiences amazing intuitive synchronicities and harmonic balance – as if all the stars were aligning to support the moment in which One was experiencing life. Coincidences happen with regular familiarity and divine serendipity. One can't explain it – things just work or fall into place with an unexplainable effortlessness. This shifted centredness, together with the practice of being virtuous, establishes a prosperity platform for living a spiritually aligned and awakened life.

Virtues

What are virtues?

Virtues are inner qualities held within One's mind-body. They are used as a principal source for guiding One's mind-body's thoughts, actions and behaviours.

There are seven identified primary universal virtues. The seven primary virtues are a gateway to experiencing One's spiritual states. They are compassion, helpfulness, acceptance, simplicity, patience, generosity and openness.

Three of these virtues accurately mirror the teachings of Lao Tzu, who says:

> I have just three things to teach: simplicity, patience, compassion. These three are your greatest treasures.

Lao Tzu's overall work was about assisting others to focus their mind-body on the beingness of living and approach life by cultivating mindfulness and using prime universal virtues as a daily practice.

To practice a virtue or multiple virtues in One's daily life is to align One's mind-body to a spiritual state. For example, if One practices compassion, One will be aligning One's mind-body to One's inner spiritual state of knowing. By being in alignment with this virtue, One is freely acting out of selflessness and demonstrating kindness to oneself and other people. One will naturally choose to help oneself, other people or animals to either meet One's transitory needs or encourage One to move beyond these needs to seek a spiritual pathway of enlightenment. One is not focusing on One's own needs, wants and desires for One's selfish benefit to the detriment of others in One's life. One is investing One's life energy by co-creating or reconfiguring reality to support the manifestation of a new occurrence in One's life or other people's lives. One is acting with intentional benefit to positively change the current situation to improve or alter the living outcome for another person or sentient Being. One is also helping in the transformation of another entity and, by doing so, it better enables One's divine purpose here on Earth now. Through this selfless act, One is actualising One's own divine purpose – being One with the universe.

To align with One's spiritual states of being, use the following discussion as a guide.

Knowing – Compassionate

Be compassionate to others to align One's mind–body to a knowing state of being. Demonstrate a loving-kindness to people in One's mind–body time of need, want or desire (without creating intentional self-harm, disharmony or conflict). What One does in this moment counts in One's life and in the lives of other people, so adopt a non-judgemental, non-resistant and non-attachment approach, no matter what the condition or circumstances. Simply respond appropriately given the presenting issue, need, want, desire, pain, frustration, anxiety or suffering. Without reward, be a self-advocate for random acts of loving-kindness in every aspect of One's life.

Awareness – Helpful

Be helpful to all to align One's mind–body to an awareness state of being. Live in service so that One's acts of helpfulness enable selfless awareness in life. Be aware that in co-creating and manifesting intended outcomes, One directly and indirectly benefits all. With awareness of One's being, One will be able to perceive how to help and serve humanity and all living things. Whatever the occurrence or opportunity, begin with self-helpfulness. Awareness of all things is to be aware of One's inner truth and spirit.

Oneness – Accepting

Be accepting to align One's mind-body to a oneness state of being. Acceptance is key to experiencing the Oneness of the universe. We are all One within – everyone is One. Prior to manifesting any change in One's current life, One will first need to accept life in its current manifestation. Accept all situations, personal circumstances and conditions as they are now and not how One's mind believes they should be, could be or might be. Without fear or favour, accept every situation, event or activity as it presents itself to One as part of One's life path. Everything is a learning and every challenge is an opportunity to transcend. Use everything in One's life for One's own transformation. Remember that this is not about approval or condoning of unpleasantness, violence or unreasonable behaviours or actions by others. First accept – then act without expectation to manifest an intentional outcome in One's life or the lives of others.

Free will – Simple

Be simple to align One's mind-body to a free will state of being. Approach work, play, relationships, life and living moments with simplicity in mind-body. Journey along the path of spiritual enlightenment and process of awakening with inner intuitiveness. The simple answers to life and living are almost always the best. Rise above the conformities of separateness and global divisiveness. Enjoy life unfolding effortlessly as One lives it. Free One's mind of attachment and fear, declutter One's living environment, home and workplace. Like a raindrop falling from the sky or a bee collecting nectar from a flower, let things simply be as they are. Live life simply – and so it will be!

CIRCLE OF MINDFUL AND CONSCIOUS EXISTENCE

Being virtuous creates an alignment to
One's spiritual consciousness and the universe

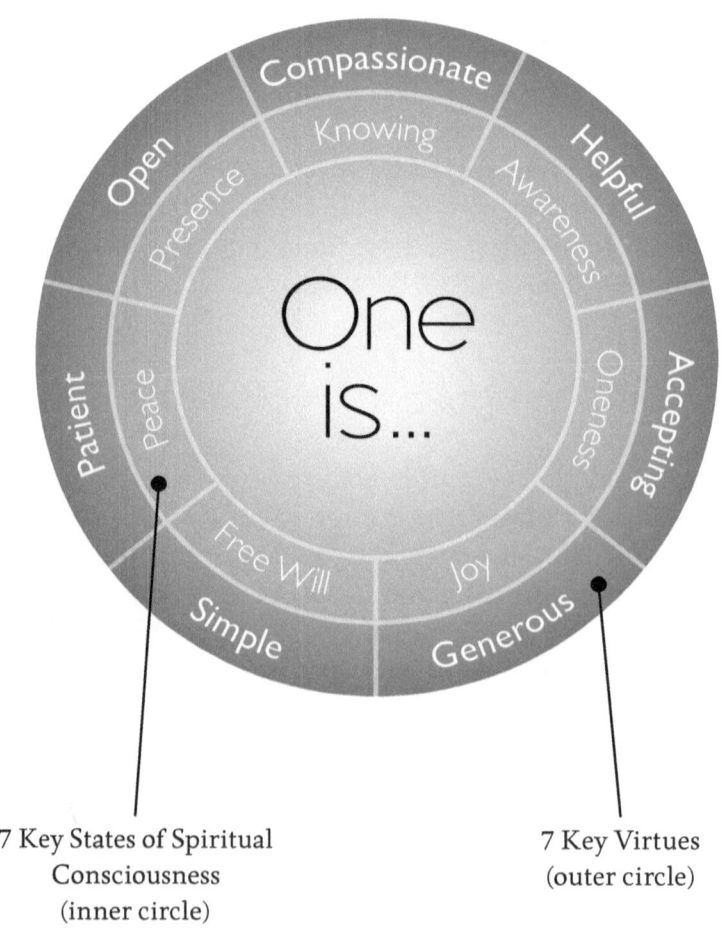

7 Key States of Spiritual
Consciousness
(inner circle)

7 Key Virtues
(outer circle)

Peace – Patient

Be patient to align One's mind–body to a peaceful state of being. Whatever moment One is in now, allow things to unfold effortlessly and naturally in harmony with the universe. Resist trying to direct the river of One's life, simply embrace the flow of life as it is. Trust in the divine timing of the universe in which all things are happening. Do nothing and spring comes. Be patient and the tide comes in naturally. Wherever One is, peace lives within One's inner being. It is an eternal state in the universe – it exists within One too. Patience is quiet, unassuming and calm in mind.

Joy – Generous

Be generous to align One's mind–body to a joyful state of being. Without expectation, give consciously of oneself – this includes One's time, thoughts of gratitude and thankfulness, energy, loving-kindness and resources. Remember that joy is at the deepest level of expressive contentment within One's spirit and life on Earth. Joy is a forever state of One's being, it exists above all the transient fun times and happy experiences. Joy is not conditional on what One has or doesn't have in One's life. Joy is ever present within One – so, give grateful thanks in every aspect of One's life. Wherever One goes in life, bring One's inner joy with One in every step, breath and moment.

Presence – Open

Be open to aligning One's mind–body to a present state of being. Engage with life and live it with an open mind towards all people, places, new opportunities, relationships and human experiences. See situations for what they truly are, without filtering or creating false images in One's mind. Bring a sense of openness to each and every conversation. Open One's mind and free One's spirit. Centre oneself within One's spiritual consciousness. Let the radiant light of One's being shine brightly and be an inspiration for everyone in the world with One's spiritual presence. Be and live in the present moment; it is One's greatest gift to oneself and others.

Living One's inner way now

Suggestions for putting the learnings, teachings and pointings of this chapter into practice in One's daily life:

- Simply accept that One is and will always be an immortal, eternal, and infinite spiritual Being of the universe. One is powerful beyond measure and an integral part of the divine oneness from which all things were created. One exists within an endless continuum of beingness or seven states of consciousness beyond space and time.
- Realise that One is a divine spirit having a human experience and not a human having a spiritual experience. One as spirit need not be anybody, go anywhere, or do anything. One is already whole and does not need to want something in order to attain everything within One's life now. One as spirit is enough.
- Be aware that One's spiritual essence is imbued with seven states of spiritual consciousness at any moment within the universe. These states are: knowing, awareness, oneness, joy, free will, peace and presence.
- Create space and time in One's life to slow down, so One can take a deep breath, relax and let go of the illusion that One's ego is in control. One is not in

control of One's external life, in the same way that One is not in control of the weather, the moon, the stars or the sun. However, One does have the capacity to influence, change and manifest One's mind–body, life and living experiences. While One's ego may perceive it is in control, this is just an illusion of relativities. The paradox here is that One does possess the potential and capability to change anything in One's life, because One is always living in a realm of infinite possibilities.

- Everything is occurring in the 'Now'. There is no past or future, except for One's mind's perception of it, so, the 'Now' of One's living experience is able to be changed. Mindful intention, together with an unequivocal trust in One's spirit, life and the universe, are key to co-creating a new life and living experiences. Know One's spirit so that One may guide One's mind–body to where it needs to be. All things happen when they need to happen – everything unfolds and is present in One's life when it occurs. Everything is on time and there is a time for everything.
- Accept – Allow – Align. Be present with One's intention and trust One's way in the universe. Move effortlessly and as easily as fresh water flowing in a river to the ocean or a gentle summer breeze across the land.

CHAPTER 2

Knowing
One's Divine Spirit

Being One now

William Shakespeare, one of literature's greatest playwrights, is famous for these lines in the play *Hamlet*:

To be or not to be: that is the question.

These words hold a clue to knowing oneself and One's spirit. To know that One's spiritual consciousness exists within a continuum of infinite beingness in the universe is essential for creating a positive understanding and compassionate spiritual relationship with One's spirit. One cannot seek or find One's spirit by looking for this divinity in a Supreme Being, the Creator, God, Allah, Krishna, a guru, Master or any entity external to oneself, as it exists within One now. All that One seeks is a reflection of what One's mind perceives One needs, thinks and feels that is missing in One's life. One is enough – being spirit or One.

In a free will state of consciousness, One is able to choose where One will ultimately be in the universe – existing as pure consciousness (One or spirit) or as a spirit host to One's mind-body.

Wherever One is, One has a responsibility to oneself to be completely there, to be fully present in the moment and to be living an awakened life.

His Holiness, the 14th Dalai Lama, born Lhamo Thondup, a well-known international refugee, 1989 Nobel Peace Prize recipient, world speaker, peace/non-violence advocate, spiritual leader and Buddhist teacher, says of spiritual accountability to oneself that:

> We must take direct responsibility for our own spiritual lives and rely upon nobody and nothing ... If another being were able to save us, surely he would already have done so? It is time, therefore, that we help ourselves.

For each person to know One's spirit, first a person must help oneself to realise One's spiritual path is within oneself and not something to be attained externally through dogma, ritual or religious rites of passage.

Carl Jung says:

> People will do anything, no matter how absurd, to avoid facing their own souls [spirits].

It is estimated that most people currently living on Earth today – over 7.5 billion people – do not know One's spirit or any idea of One's divine spiritual consciousness. A surprising number of humans believe that One is simply an individual with thoughts, beliefs, desires and dreams. One's mind sees oneself as being defined as a body with a mind, which is filling or occupying a certain space and place in life. The majority of men, women and children have been socialised into belonging to or being part of a particular group, tribe, culture or profession and being assigned a specific individual identity within a community, society, First Nation or nation-state. There exists an intentional intergenerational silence about not speaking about One's spirit and One's inner oneness. One's inner connection and alignment to the divine oneness of the universe is seen as an external concept that only applies to people who are seeking an alternative lifestyle that goes against mainstream modern society or contemporary religious beliefs. The conversation about living in the present moment and knowing One's spirit on an intimate level is viewed by many as a hypothetical and distant construct that has no purpose in One's daily life, family or community. However, there has never been a more important moment in One's life to know One's spirit through aligning with the divine Source of the universe. It is of paramount importance that each and every generation of humans reconfigures One's life and living presence to enable the transfer of this divine perception as something awesome, amazing and a wondrous part of One's inner wellbeing and spiritual life.

One's knowing of One's spirit needs to be experienced in the moment and in a very intimate, personal and private way. To know spirit is to be in touch with One's inner presence in all aspects of One's life. It should not be viewed as a distant thing far out in the universe, to be attained as a reward from a benevolent divine being for living through and surviving times of great hardship, pain and suffering. To know One's spirit, One need only to look within oneself. Spirit is always within One – it has no place to go but to be with One for eternity. To reach a profound knowing and understanding of One's spirit, One need only be still, silent and present. One's inner presence is something that lives within One at each and every moment of One's life.

Many people cloud One's mind not knowing spirit by following One's egoic mindless thought patterns and self-limiting behaviours in daily life. Letting go of control and expanding this narrowness opens One's mind to experiencing spiritual moments of alignment in One's life. People who operate with an egoic mindset are not centred within One's spirit or particularly aligned to any of One's states of spiritual consciousness. This is an unawake person. That is okay. There are many millions of unawake people on Earth who are living an unconscious way of life without ever knowing that One is living this way. It is like being on autopilot as a human being or living in a dreamlike state of reality. The lights are on, but no One is home. To live like this, One will be totally mind-centred in One's thoughts, beliefs and actions. It will feel as if One is simply going through the motions of life without any mindful direction or meaningful purpose. One's default direction in life will be to experience an ego-centric journey until One awakens within. To live with an awakened consciousness, One must realise One's divinity through knowing One's spirit. However, if One is unawake, One may be living One's life as a complete delusion in order to hide from One's own spiritual self-truth. One may be living life principally according to the constructed illusions of false truths that have reinforced and validated One's mind's identity, personhood and social conditioning.

Unawake people believe that One's mind is acting within the human experience because One's mind sees it as One's mind–body only source of physical sensory input or reference point in the universe. Spiritual consciousness is far too much of an intangible and abstract concept of existence for One's egoic mind to come to terms with or realise. One's mind–body experiences are just like guests visiting One's house or divine dwelling. All thoughts, feelings and sensory inputs only occupy the human mind–body for a limited moment in space and time. What comes to One will eventually leave One's human experience too – nothing is permanent in this life.

The truth is that One is spirit. As this spirit, One is host to mind–body experiences. This is the reality of One's true existence as a spiritual entity on Earth.

Let's take a brief moment to examine this interesting question: 'What does One know for certain about life and the experience of living it?'

This is a tremendously powerful and reflective question to consider.

When One is able to deeply reflect upon this question within the omnipresence of One's Being, One has the ability to actually destroy One's identity, personhood (residual image of oneself) and the false constructs with which this world has been created. One is able to dissolve the illusions of the self within One's mind. One is able to come to a new knowing of reality. One realises that the world One has created in One's mind is all a false truth. In the words of Buddha, 'All is an illusion'. One has principally relied upon and lived a life based on a diverse range of secondhand assumptions, beliefs, behaviours, opinions and perceptions from family, friends, groups, community, society and nation. Through mindfulness meditation and appreciative inquiry, One is able to deconstruct the world that One has constructed for One's mind–body. Thought by thought, One is able to come to terms with the idea that the life One's mind thought One was living is just part of an echo or ripple of humanity's collective continuity. What emerges now is clarity that One's spiritual consciousness has been masked by a mind–body dreamlike experience. One thought arises and that is: 'One is a Being of infinite knowing'.

To One who is truly awake, the dream illusion of mind–body is obvious. To all others, it is accepted as real because One's mind only perceives One point of view in this world – which is from One's mind–body experience.

Know that One is this 'Infinite Knowing'. It is not a practice, but rather the constant recognition of what already exists within oneself now.

There are no preconditions for One to align to this state of knowing within One's spiritual consciousness. One simply surrenders to the certainty of this existence without judgement, attachment or resistance.

The certainty of knowing is found in the non-dependency on time, form (altered consciousness) and fixed thoughts. Eckhart Tolle says:

> To offer no resistance to life is to be in a state of grace, ease, and lightness. This state is then no longer dependent upon things being in a certain way, good or bad. It seems almost paradoxical, yet when your inner dependency on form is gone, the general conditions of your life, the outer forms, tend to improve greatly. Things, people, or conditions that you thought you needed for your happiness now come to you with no struggle or effort on your part, and you are free to enjoy and appreciate them – while they last. All those things, of course, will still pass away, cycles will come and go, but with dependency gone there is no fear of loss anymore. Life flows with ease.

To be totally present now is to know One's spirit and flow effortlessly with grace and ease in One's life. In a state of knowing, all answers come to One. One is intuitively guided to where One needs to be in the universe.

Spirit speaks in silence

Just because One breathes, doesn't mean One needs to speak. The same can be said of the sky – just because there are clouds, doesn't mean it will rain. As a living entity, One is host to mind, but it doesn't mean that One should always think. No mind or no thought is a natural condition of simply being in this world.

One's mind may struggle and feel anxious about doing nothing at first, but give oneself time to let go, get comfortable and adjust to being present in the moment. At times, the thoughts in One's mind may feel like a noisy flock of squawking galahs or cockatoos all trying to be heard. But in time, and with a little patience, this will all become white noise and eventually fade into the background.

When One uses mindful meditation practices, One is able to become self-aware and eventually self-manage the diversity of thoughts in One's mind when they arise. Mindfully meditating for as little as twenty minutes a day will create a healthy habit and provide lasting, positive residual effects for One's entire mind–body. There is a lot of research that supports the idea that participating in daily meditation sessions, combined with regular exercise, increases and contributes to One's overall individual wellness and personal wellbeing. Meditation will enable One to guide One's mind to a place of serene calmness, silent stillness and quiet tranquillity. As no thought in the mind becomes the 'norm' or normal operating system for One's life, a wave of peaceful resonance or coherence will be generated within the brain. When this occurs, One will have the capacity to change One's brainwaves and remodulate the biochemistry of One's entire human body in this spiritual sacred space of silence.

Being comfortable with silence is about accepting and allowing free space to be present in One's life. Space between people allows One to be as One chooses to be. Space within any conversation allows time to breathe, to listen, to reflect, to consider, to ponder, to wonder and to absorb. Space is vital for good communication between all people and an important quality within relationships. If there were no space, there would be no life. Space is vital and necessary for all things to manifest in life. First create the space, then allow the right causes and conditions to occur naturally and effortlessly to enable any and all manifestations in the universe.

Mooji says:

> Just stay open allowing what is being said to simply be heard in the consciousness without taking particular hold of any thought or idea such as what to do with what is being heard; let the listening just 'happen', as it were. You are there behind the listening mind.

Do not lose oneself in the context of the conversation or get carried away with One's own worries, concerns, fears, cravings, anger, frustration or desires. Free One's mind of any intent other than to be present and open in the moment. By staying in silence, One is giving the gift of space, and in this space lies One's freedom. Freedom to choose and freedom to simply let things be just as they are meant to be. This is an act of loving-kindness between oneself and another spiritual being. It is a simple and yet divinely profound gesture that need not aim to prove anything, as One's vibrational energies are shared together. Listening in silence and being completely present in One's mind–body–spirit is a powerful quality that is often underestimated.

Silence is the Source of all spiritual knowing. If One surrenders to the silence within One's spirit, One will awaken to an inner awareness that is beyond anything that One will ever experience outside of One's mind–body. In this realm of no words, no thoughts, no concepts, no senses, no desires, no noise and no mind, there is only the immutability of divine and eternal serenity.

It is a beingness of conscious bliss in the universe, ever present in every aspect of One's daily life, from the time One wakes up in the morning, throughout the day, until One finally falls asleep at night. The soft subtlety of silence is spiritually present wherever One is in life. When One finally surrenders to this realisation, One will be able to embrace the abundance of infinite silence and the unlimited space that precedes every manifestation in the universe.

In silence, know One's infinite freedom within.

To be silent is to bring oneself closer to One's spirit. It is from this place that One is able to think more clearly, act more virtuously and be more present in One's life and with others. Being silent does not mean that One is absent from the conversation or life. One's mind is just listening without judgement. One need not respond to everything that comes to One. If it comes – let it. If it goes – let it. Just like standing at the water's edge on a sandy beach. As One stands in complete silence, simply allow the waves to come and wash gently over One's feet while still observing the motion of the waves. Do not speak, just observe the waves and One's breathing – in and out, then in and out again. Know that One needs to do nothing but be present in this moment. Just be, without expectation or distraction. In this silence, allow One's mind to be still, calm and peaceful – just breathe and observe.

In stillness, One's spirit speaks, not in words or particular mind–body sensations but in an intuitive voice, a quietness that is soft, gentle and aligned to higher self. Accessing universal wisdom, truth, reality and a future vision or outcome is a passive process of alignment of One's mind with One's inner being or states of consciousness and the universe. There is no road map or any fixed steps of spiritual certainty to this place of centredness. Simply create a space that will allow One's mind to be quiet and still within itself. Centre oneself in the moment; do not be distracted by things, the situation or thoughts. If a thought arises, simply acknowledge it, then let it go again. Allow any thought that arises to dissolve back into the abyss of nothingness it came from. Hold no attachment to thought, no resistance to thought or the relevance of its importance in One's life. Come to this space with no agenda to take action or no action. Simply be mindful, restful and present in the space and situation as it is occurring.

Mindfulness is as much a practice of letting go as it is about centring oneself within One's mind and aligning with One's spirit.

Without judgement, attachment or resistance, be present when One's mind is actively in a mode of being silent, observing, perceiving and intending. Allow thoughts, words, people and places to manifest as they are and not how One's mind wants them to be. It takes practice to train and discipline One's mind in a gentle, kind and compassionate way. To be still is a learned practice, or habit, that can be achieved anywhere, in any place and at any time. When One is master of One's mind,

One has achieved a great mastery of being still using nothing but silence. When One is beginning mindful meditation practices, it may at first feel very strange, as if One should be doing something, or that One is all alone in the world. Do not worry or be concerned. This is simply One's ego trying to justify its own crazy logic that One's mind must be active at all times with thought otherwise it has no purpose or value in One's life. Know that all these feelings within One's mind and with oneself will soon pass, as surely as clouds moving across the sky. Have faith in oneself and One's spiritual existence. This is where One's truth resides.

When sitting or standing quietly, place One's hand on One's heart, in the centre of One's chest (One may also close One's eyes), and know that One is ever present within One's spirit. Say to oneself, 'One is here, as spirit – within One'. 'One is now.' 'One is present.' Remember that One is host to One's mind and body. One also knows that One is One's own truth and inner light. Within this truth, One is a witness to all that is in this moment. One is free and One is eternally safe now and forever. During these moments, be silent and allow wisdom to arise from within. Be observant as One accepts the truth as it shows and reveals itself. Be perceptive as reality manifests as it will be in One's life. Be intentionally intuitive within and trust the universe to guide One. Trust One's vision to co-create the best version of oneself and manifest One's living outcome. Believe and let One's life unfold with divine purpose. Be silent … be still and allow One's spirit to speak to One in this forever moment of now.

Intuitive insight

When One realises One is spirit and awakens to One's divine consciousness, One will know that this is the infinite presence within One that One has been searching for all along. Eckhart Tolle says:

> Even if you achieve your outer purpose, it will never satisfy you if you haven't found your inner purpose, which is awakening, being present, being in alignment with life. True power comes out of the presence; it is the presence.

Know that wherever One's spirit goes in life, One is home. Simply by being One with oneself is enough in life. One's ego may seek and search for more proof to validate its artificial identity in the external world, but nothing will ever satisfy this misguided mission. Many millions of people all around the world search for years – even an entire lifetime – looking for the right teacher, guru or Master who has the right words or faith-based practices to give One advice, information or referrals. It is common for a diversity of people across all sorts of different cultures, communities, First Nations and countries to seek daily guidance on how to learn the right way to eat, sleep, work, think, pray, love and live. Some lucky people find One's inner way in shared experiences with partners, friends, kin or family. Others repeat patterns of dysfunctional dependency based on external satisfaction, hoping that something external to oneself is going to make them whole or bring pure joy and bliss into One's life. Finally, there are light warriors who have the courage, honesty and vision to look inside oneself to discover One's divinity, radiance and beauty along One's spiritual journey flowing with 'the way' of the universe.

Wherever One is in life, the important thing to remember is that it all begins and ends at the same divine Source: One's spiritual consciousness. One can never leave home if One has never left. One will never be apart from oneself or One's spirit, no matter how hard One's mind tries to convince oneself otherwise.

The mind, in its most basic form, works as a 'human search engine', encoding and interpreting the outside world in an easily recognisable way so it can navigate, negotiate and make sense of it all. To figure out the world in which One lives, mind creates its own personal 'living operating system' to guide

One's beliefs, behaviours and relationships with things and each other. Everyone on Earth has a distinct living operating system that influences the vibrational energy of One's mind–body in the universe, while, at the same time, One's spirit is an infinite silent observer. Ever since One was born, One has been continually uploading and upgrading One's living operating system into what One could be referred to as One's personhood, character or identity. Think of oneself as being born with no mind and no thoughts. One's mind could be referred to as having a living operating system of 0.0 at the beginning of One's life. Through the stages of One's life, as One's mind–body develops and the brain grows, One creates and reconfigures infinite neural pathways in One's mind. Research indicates that the average human brain has about 100 billion neurons, or nerve cells. It is suggested that each neuron may be connected to up to 10,000 other neurons in the brain, passing signals to each other via as many as 1,000 trillion synaptic connections. This is estimated to be equivalent to a computer with a 1 trillion bit per second processor. Estimates vary wildly, but the human brain's memory capacity may be from 1 to 1,000 terabytes of information or more.

Over time, One's mind receives a vast number of images, thoughts and interactive learning experiences each and every day. All these inputs significantly contribute to shaping, changing and configuring the neural synapses within One's brain. By changing One's thoughts, One changes One's vibrational energy in the world – it's only natural that the universe responds accordingly to these new vibrations (positive or negative). Throughout the course of One's life, One has multiple personal living operating systems that One's mind uses at different stages of One's life to engage, explore and actively live in this world. One's living operating system as a child (v1.0) is not necessarily the same version when One is a teenager (v2.0), young adult (v3.0) or adult (v4.0). One's mind–body is continually changing over the course of One's life. However, One's spirit or spiritual consciousness remains a constant in One's life right through One's formative years of mind–body growth, development and construction of One's collective personhood.

Marianne Williamson, American author, spiritual leader and political activist, says:

> Nothing binds you except your thoughts; nothing limits you except your fears; and nothing controls you except your beliefs.

Mind uses the outside landscape to inform its inside mindscape of beliefs, thoughts and behaviours. A continual feedback loop exists within mind, so it can affirm a certainty principle about the world that it imagines and creates and where One's mind–body now exists. The mind is particularly clever about seeking out, selectively summarising and solidifying streams of constructed beliefs from sensory mind–body inputs and patterns in One's life. Mind is also preconditioned to manifest a fundamental basic belief that requires it to externally validate its existence and identity. It is something that resides in all Beings. In expressing and applying this certainty principle to create a stable world, One's mind uses the process of daily living or specially designed meaningful journeys to continually inform itself. An egoic mind manifests the illusion that mistakenly makes One's mind think that by taking 'you' on a journey it is the real architect of One's life – and therefore mind must be the master, to the exclusion of oneself (spirit).

Survival of the human species relies upon people and cultures validating specific and certain thoughts. When One's mind–body is part of a family, friend-kinship network or community, it creates an enabling environment for One's mind–body to be nurtured in a particular way. This is where One's mind is able to affirm and validate newly constructed realities. One's mind will cycle through countless tests to validate particular thoughts over the course of One's entire life. It can be said that

One's human experiences are as much a product of the living process as they are about being able to apply a process to living. The egoic mind seeks the simulating sensation of seeking. This is how it sustains its separateness from spirit, and it is fiercely resistant to surrendering the illusion of control and certainty. The idea of letting go and just 'being' is such an unknown and abstract concept that an egoic mind's first response is to react and respond with overwhelming fear. This is understandable, because an egoic mind cannot find something that is beyond searching and within beingness itself.

'Beingness' requires the mind only to be still. In this stillness, let life unfold around One with ease and effortlessness. It will require a sustained commitment to mindful meditation practice, but this will be worth it in the end. Eventually One will be able to sit in quiet contentment and peaceful 'no mind' contemplation anywhere in the world.

The easiest way to tap into One's own personal mindfulness meditation session is to focus on One's breathing. Sit in a comfortable position, close One's eyes and centre One's focus on One's chest and One's breathing. Allow oneself to just be in the space and breathe. Notice how the air comes into One's body and then release it slowly, calmly and patiently. All One has to focus on is: one breath, one moment – now. Take one simple breath, stay with this one moment and be present now. Repeat this cycle for twenty minutes or until One is centred within One's beingness. One does not need to be anywhere else in the world or the universe. All One needs to know is how to take one simple breath – now. Stay in the moment of this breath for as long as possible and everything else in One's mind will naturally fall away. Stay within the space of One's chest, rising and falling as One breathes in and breathes out. In being in this space, One also aligns to the infinite knowingness of One's inner spirit.

Knowledge and knowing

Let's take a moment to explore the vast difference between knowledge and knowing. Everyone has knowledge of something or other at some point in One's life, but not all realise One's intuitive knowing within One's spirit. In simple terms, knowledge is mind-centred. It focuses on One's mind's capacity and ability to access and use acquired information. Over time, One's knowledge bank grows and changes by attaining additional personal learnings or self-selecting particular experiences in the world. The traditional use of the word 'know' in this context relates primarily to the use of One's mind of this accumulation of information, ideas, concepts or practices.

One understands just how important it is to 'know' how to effectively operate and function in the world today. The proper and efficient use of living knowledge stored in the memory centre of One's brain is a critical social skillset that is necessary for One's basic survival. Applying this knowledge correctly helps One to distinguish between friend or foe, live off Country (land, sea and sky), navigate the natural environment or negotiate a successful pathway in life. It is One of the most fundamental tools for self-preservation and the continued existence of all humans on Earth. Without the transmission of knowledge through individual memes or specific thoughts within a culture or society, it would be impossible for a generation to pass One's collective teachings, learning, pointings and survival skills on to the next generation. Individual human knowledge is continually adapting to the present moment within One's mind–body and can be consciously altered at any moment over the course of One's life.

The other aspect of human knowledge is directly coded into One's DNA. This also changes over time as well, through individual gene modulation.

Mooji says:

> True knowledge means to be empty; empty of identity and belief in and attachment to psychological conditioning. There is great space and silence here in the emptiness.

Mooji is referring to the place of knowing or spiritual intuition within One's spirit. That 'gut feeling' when One knows something is about to happen, or that funny feeling inside One's body that One needs to do something, select a certain pathway or even create space in this moment to connect with someone in person or on the phone or via a smartphone app like Facebook Messenger, FaceTime, WhatsApp, Teams or Zoom. It surprises One how often that One feels like this lately, especially when One is empty of any egoic thoughts, concerns or fears. Things just come to One naturally without any effort. This state of knowing exists within all Beings, not just in those who choose to follow a spiritual path or enlightenment journey.

A good way to access One's infinite state of knowing is to centre oneself in One's spiritual presence. The easiest way to do this is to let go of all the thoughts and images in One's mind. Lao Tzu says:

> Empty yourself of everything – let the mind become still.

When One's mind is free of knowledge, One is able to access the infinite space of knowing within oneself and the universe. With mindful practice and thoughtful habits, One can be guided intuitively by One's spirit in every aspect of One's life. One simply flows in alignment with the day, things appear before One, and One is more centred, calm and confident. There will always be personal challenges in One's life, but by being spirit-centred, One will know One's way in the world within each and every breath, step and moment.

One will know when to begin things and when to stop. One will sense how to uncomplicate One's life and see into the heart of the matter with loving-kindness, compassion and simplicity.

One will also know within oneself when it is time to pause, rest and recover or when to press on to achieve a selfless task or move on with One's personal journey in life. One will know the reasons One is here now.

To know suffering in One's life is also the means by which One can free One's life of it. Buddha consistently says:

> I teach only suffering and the transformation of suffering.

When One recognises One's own suffering in One's life, One should view this touchstone as a gift and be grateful for the opportunity to look more closely at it. When One looks into the heart of One's suffering, One will discover what has brought this situation into One's life at this particular moment. Through closer investigation of One's pain and suffering, One can create a solution and find a way that will dissolve it completely by transforming it into peace, joy and freedom.

The definition of 'suffer' is the state of undergoing pain, distress, or hardship. The path of suffering was the means by which the Buddha used to rise above it. By aligning to One's divine higher self, it is also a way to be free now as well.

Everyone at some point in One's life has experienced pain, but not all people have endured suffering. If One has experienced the burning pains of hunger with no food, the freezing chills of winter without warmth, the sweltering heat of summer without shade or water, the loss of family or friends without a place to live or call home, the feeling of illness and not being well, or the ravages of being in a conflict situation or disharmonious relationship and not feeling safe or loved, One will appreciate the value of the simple elements like food, water, shelter, love and companionship. One is very grateful for these simple things in One's life, like good food to eat, clothes and shoes, a cup of clean water, family and friends, a place to stay, being well, and feeling safe and loved.

One remembers growing up in a tent in Mt Colah, north of Sydney, and living for a brief time beside a burnt out fibro timber house in the bush, which the family moved into prior to shifting into a 'proper house' in the suburbs. While the conditions were not ideal, One did not feel that One was suffering, as One had the love, connection and security of One's family. One was lucky. One also was very accepting of these conditions as it was all that One knew at the time.

With 'no self' know oneself

There is no greater beauty to behold in the universe than knowing One's own spirit or Being. It is one of the greatest turning points in One's life when One realises 'who One is now'. At this moment and in this realisation, it shatters One's residual self-image within One's mind completely. It will feel as if One's existing, stable and well-crafted perception of oneself has been broken into a million pieces or that One has totally fallen apart. Do not be afraid; it is all part of the process of letting go and deconstructing years or even decades of false beliefs about oneself. Beyond this moment, know that there is no way of returning to One's previous persona. One simply needs to accept that One is in a different space and place of One's life now. One has ascended to a changed reality of light and truth from which to experience a new way of living and being now.

One may have previously carefully constructed an intricate network of beliefs about One's self-image or personhood, but this is of little value to One who finally realises the truth within oneself. One will truly be in awe, wondering how this can be. How can there be such a divine light, spiritual Being, warrior angel or 'Bright' with such magnificence within One? One will know it for the very first time – again.

It is something that One has always known, but it has been hidden away from oneself by One's very own egoic thoughts within One's mind. One might even say to oneself: 'One always knew it, One is the light within oneself, One is eternal, One always had a sense of this eventuality. One finally has the clarity of One's own truth. There is something about this experience that feels so right, comfortable and familiar.'

When looking for direction and guidance in One's life, Eckhart Tolle says:

> Stop looking outside for scraps of pleasure or fulfillment – you have a treasure within that is infinitely greater than anything the world can offer.

One of the hardest things in life is letting go of what One's egoic mind thinks is real, especially when it comes to One's own individual self-image. Many people invest in trying to project an image on social media to others that will conform with the conditioning of contemporary thoughts merely to please others, feel accepted and be socially validated by friends, family, work colleagues and the community in which One lives. When One is more concerned about what others think of oneself, One gives up One's own power and mindful centre to be present within oneself. Being mindful of One's thoughts and centred within One's spirit is the key to living a life of joy in this present moment.

One of the greatest living principles of life is attributed to Tilopa, an India tantric practitioner who embodied and cultivated psychic and spiritual abilities and powers. Tilopa promoted the idea for One to create and configure One's mind to be:

> Open to everything and attached to nothing.

This is such a simple statement and yet it is incredibly powerful when put into practice on a daily basis. If One is to incorporate this practice principle into One's normal living habits, One will need to create space in One's life to review and reflect on One's current thought patterns and thinking processes.

Ask oneself these simple questions:

- How does One currently perceive oneself and One's residual self-image?
- Does One engage with the world One lives in from an ego perspective and ask 'What's in it for me?' or from a spirit perspective and ask 'How can One help?'

When One's desire for truth outweighs One's mind's fear of change, One makes a mindful decision to align with One's spirit rather than a closed egoic mind.

To change the narrative of One's experiences and vibrations, One must shine a light on the darkness of One's ego in mind and the suffering caused by One's attachment to fear, unworthiness, illness, negativity, hate, bitterness, resentment, unkindness, loneliness, jealousy, envy, greed, desire, expectation, separateness and judgement. It is important to use these moments of suffering to teach oneself about how One can rise above these challenging circumstances and create higher vibrational energy by being open to everything and attached to nothing in One's life.

Know that One is a great co-creator in the universe. One has the ability to change any aspect of One's life. One's manifested reality is simply the universe reflecting back to One what One is already creating through One's existing beliefs and thoughts (consciously or unconsciously).

Being mindful of One's way of living will give oneself the opportunity to make conscious decisions that align with One's spirit in every waking moment of One's life. No matter what is happening in One's life or relationships, be spirit-centred and respond with compassion, gratitude and loving-kindness. This is the mark of One's spiritual maturity and true self-mastery. It clearly shows others that One has accepted the challenge to remove the 'self' from the equation of One's life and be present in the moment.

If One is still automatically reacting, being triggered or emotionally responsive to situations or circumstances in negative ways, this is an indication that One is still clinging to One's residual self-image and egoic attachment to specific toxic thought streams or particular poisonous patterns. One requires time to heal One's mind–body so One can detox One's mind and cleanse One's body of this temporary misalignment or dysfunctional harmony. Do not underestimate One's inner power to completely heal oneself and be free now. Know that egoic thoughts are only temporary, because One's natural state is to be well and aligned to One's spirit, positive energy and highest vibration. One will not be able to manifest a different lifestyle or living experiences if One does not first change from within. The universe can only reflect to One what One continually chooses to be in this moment.

Say this to oneself, on a daily basis to shift One's inner energy and increase One's positive vibrations in One's life:

> One is a wonderful, beautiful and loving sentient Being. One radiates infinite love and light out into the universe. One can achieve anything in this life. The universe is always on One's side. One accepts that everything is okay. One surrenders to the universe and flows effortlessly with life. One lives and experiences an amazing, awesome and abundant life. Things naturally work out for One, as they are supposed to. Opportunities just appear to One. The resources of the universe are available to One. Good things easily and spontaneously come to One. One is grateful for everyone and everything in One's life – here and now.

Within mindful intention lives the potential for One to manifest anything in One's life with the cooperation of other sentient Beings on the planet. When One lets go of 'the self' or One's artificial identity, One will be able to align and know One's true spirit within. It is important to know that there is no distance that separates oneself from One's divine spirit.

Everything that One experiences in life is neutral and devoid of meaning. It is only in One's mind that One attaches a label to the experience and defines it as a particular thing (good or bad). One's reality is shaped by One's matrix of belief systems and filtered through the lenses of One's emotions (thoughts and feelings). Learn to recognise how One's mind is and how its perception affects One's interpretation of people, places and personal activities.

When One consciously lets go of 'the self', One will be able to allow outside circumstances to simply be as they are without needing to label the experience. One will be able to stay aligned within One's spirit and grounded in One's state of beingness. One will have no need or desire for things to be a certain way, as One will not seek the outside world to change to conform to One's internal expectation of the event, activity or circumstance. One will not need any situation to validate One's inner mental perception of it or oneself because, with no self, it does not need to be socially validated. One is simply allowing oneself to be present in the moment when it is occurring. One is detached from the experience and engaged in it at the same time. This may seem like a paradox at first, but it is a sign of One's ability to move easily through this world and not be a mental prisoner of One's thoughts and beliefs.

One's inner expression of joy, peace and awareness is not conditional on any external reality in front of One. This is because One is centred within One's spirit and chooses to be One's true and authentic self. One is naturally peaceful, joyful, adaptable, creative and empowering as infinite existence in this 'Now' moment. With 'no self' One is then able to know One and be One now.

Awakening to One's awareness

Know that there is nothing to do, nowhere to go, no program to study nor agenda to follow in order for One to be aware of who One is now. Simply be still, silent and allow everything to fall away from One's mind–body in mindful meditation and fall into place in One's life at the same time. Be aware that there is nothing to be attained in meditation, only the opportunity to lose everything that One's mind perceives it has already acquired. With no-mind, One is able to bring great clarity to oneself and One's life by being One with the oneness within One now. Nothing needs to be added as One is already enough, whole and complete. Does a flower have to do something to be a flower? No, it need only be itself in this present moment. The purpose of a flower is simply to be a flower. The same can be said of every living thing in nature and in the universe. One's purpose here on Earth is to awaken to One's infinite awareness of oneself and be true to One's authentic oneness, wherever One is now.

Awakening does not mean that 'you' as a person awakens, as there is only the awakening to a state of conscious awareness within oneself. If One continues to identify with the 'you' who is either awake or not awake, then One can say that this 'you' is still living an unconscious life.

One need not put anything in front of oneself or chase after anything in One's life. One's path is not to run away from anything or towards anything. One's joy, peace and living contentment already exists now. There is no need to strive, stress or struggle in life – just be.

Thich Nhat Hanh expresses it beautifully:

> Just being in the moment, in this place, is the deepest practice of meditation.

Too many people think that One should be continually striving and competing to acquire more money, higher social media status and exposure, more experiences or increased assets. These people believe that it is necessary for One to attain a particular income, way of life or lifestyle to be happy and fulfilled. Most people will not see that One can be completely at ease and content by living life along a pathless path. This is because this path does not meet 'normal' socially validated expectations. On the surface, this way may seem aimless, with little to no direction. However, this way of life is all about being centred within oneself. It does not matter where One is or which direction One is facing in life if One is always centred within oneself – just being at One with oneself and all.

Know that One does not need to attain a goal or live for a particular purpose in order to experience enlightenment; enlightenment already exists within One now. One need not search for it anywhere, but awaken to One's awareness of it within oneself. One does not need to live a virtuous life and practice mindful meditation to attain a higher divine position in the cosmos. When One knows that One, as spirit or spiritual consciousness, lacks nothing, One's desire to strive, compete, chase or control comes to a complete end. One is at infinite peace in this present moment.

When One is in this present moment, everything is accessible to One, even One's inner awakening, through aligning to One's infinite spiritual awareness. One's egoic mind will want to take One on a journey to justify the awakening process, as it is afraid of losing control and seeks to avoid the loss of being in charge. It will use any and all sorts of distractions, diversions and delays to justify postponing One realising One's truth in order to avoid its own dissolution. The truth is, One does not need to wait a moment longer to realise what One already knows.

To awaken is not about fixing One's personal story, such as painful relationships from the past or preparing oneself in a holy way for the future. To be awake is to free One's mind and truly see One's life journey by directly experiencing One's spiritual awareness within One's spirit. It is about saying 'yes' to living life as part of the divine realm of One's higher existence in the universe. All that One requires is total surrender to One's infinite existence and awareness in the 'Now'.

Buddha was meeting with a group of people in a new community village who were listening to his teachings for the very first time. An important official from the community gathering decided to question the words, teachings and authority of Buddha to speak on such important spiritual matters. It was this official's role to inform the people what they needed to know in the community. The official approached and asked Buddha, 'Who are 'you'?' Buddha replied, 'I am awake.'

This story is a good example of how people cling to One's identity in order to justify One's position, power and prominence in the community. When One is awake, One need not have a title, position or privileged status of power in the community in which One's lives in order to be fully engaged, awake and present in the moment.

When challenges arise in One's life, take a moment to centre oneself within One's inner peace, calmness and tranquillity. Stay in this space without attachment to any emotional thoughts and feelings, judgement of any issues, words or behaviour, or resistance to any perceived change or challenges to One's identity or personhood. Simply listen and be present in the moment. As difficult as it may seem, remain still in the eye of any external storm in One's life. Remember that all things pass eventually, including the most catastrophic moments in nature and One's life. Know that One's ego will always seek to react, attack, justify or defend itself by any means possible. One's ego would rather trigger an avalanche of disharmony and destruction in One's relationships to deflect the focus of attention on to something or someone else than face the prospect of truly looking at oneself.

One of the greatest internal mental struggles One will ever have is the daily monitoring and managing of One's mind's inner ego. In the end, One will need to 'kill off' One's ego in order to be free of it. But it will continue to remain in One's mind like liquid metal and may re-form at any time if One is not mindful and spiritually centred. The only way to be sure that ego does not significantly arise and take shape in negative, selfish or controlling ways is to train One's mind to imbue a space that does not feed ego at all. One does this by cultivating One's mindful virtues, engaging in regular meditation practices and nurturing One's spirit from a place of inner peace, oneness, balance and harmony in the world.

Being aware of One's ego is the first step in recognising its existence in One's mind. If One is mind-centred and begins an intentional selfish thought or statement with the words 'I want …', I desire …', 'I seek …' or 'I am …', it is reasonable to assume that One's ego is in effect and actively operating. It is choosing to direct One's life by trying to satisfy One's inner constructed identity, personhood or perceived direction in the world from within One's mind. The other way to recognise when the ego is in effect is that it will try and escape the present moment by retreating to the past or going to the future in One's mind. It will also not be satisfied with whatever One has in One's life – here and now. Know that One's ego is never satisfied with more of anything and yet it will mindlessly chase after it with no regard for other people, the community or the environment.

There are only two ways to alter an egoic lifestyle. The first is to be aware of it and make change within One's mind. The second is by way of the universe itself, which is always for One's higher good. The universe will manifest circumstances that will significantly alter the course of One's living experiences. Sometimes these changes to One's lifestyle are the result of a dramatic impact to One's life. These changes can often take the form of significant shifts in One's relationships, health and wellbeing. They may also dramatically affect One's day-to-day living experiences or working environments due to the loss of a partner, family member or loved One. These changes may present as an acquired mind–body illness, or an injury in the workplace or in life. When this happens, it may require One to make major or profound adjustments to One's internal mental landscape within One's mind and make other changes to One's lifestyle.

The way of the universe is to guide One on One's journey to One's higher self. It is not there to punish One for doing what One has done or has not done but to show a higher vibrational life and reflection of Source energy that is present now. Know that every problem that One sees is only a perception that resides in One's mind. With One's awareness of One's inner spirit and place in the universe, One will always be able to see a divine light in a dark world created by humans.

Mooji says:

> You are pure Awareness. You are not Awareness sometimes and sometimes not Awareness. The idea that you are only sometimes awareness and sometimes not awareness is itself an idea appearing in Awareness. Be aware of this.

Whenever life's little dramas arise during the course of One's day or in One's life, make a conscious decision to not let other people's issues, concerns or worries disturb One's inner peace. Simply align to One's awareness of what is now present in One's life and rise above it all – be the more enlightened Being. Stay centred in One's lovingly kind and compassionate vibrations, peaceful harmony and positive lifestyle. Be mindful of not being manipulated, lured or sucked into a vortex of chaos, confusion and corruption created by other people with egocentric minds and agendas. Know that One is a co-creator of One's life and destiny – make it so now.

Living One's inner way now

Suggestions for putting the learnings, teachings and pointings of this chapter into practice in One's daily life:

- In the morning, before One begins One's day on Earth, remind oneself to be One or spirit, soul or cosmic consciousness. Let this be the centrepoint of One's daily life and flow with whatever happens next.
- Make an effort to take direct responsibility for One's own spiritual realisation, awakening and life journey. Know that One is an indomitable spirit with limitless potential.
- Create space to regularly practice mindful meditation for twenty minutes per day. Take time out of One's daily routine to incorporate an activity where One can sit quietly and patiently listen in silence. This is the language of spirit.
- Remind oneself that only with 'no-self' One can know oneself. One is infinite existence and awareness.
- No matter what is happening in One's life or relationships, be spirit-centred and respond with compassion, gratitude and loving-kindness.
- Understand that enlightenment already exists within One now. One need not search for it anywhere, but awaken to One's awareness of it within oneself.
- Be aware that there is nothing to be attained in meditation, only the opportunity to lose everything which One's mind perceives it has already acquired.

CHAPTER 3

The Way
Align With Spirit, Country and the Universe

Journey to One's true path in life

It has often been said that One should trust One's journey in life. For the most part, this is a pretty positive attitude to have in One's mind to live One's life, particularly when everything appears to be flowing along as effortlessly and smoothly as a summer breeze. It is easy to feel good when good things are happening in One's life. It is reassuring to feel loved when someone is being loving towards One. It becomes more difficult to trust in life, the journey or the universe when things are not going particularly well, when things are just not working out for One. When One is confronted with an unexpected work-life challenge, dramatic life event or relationship obstacle in One's way, it may force One to seriously question One's long held beliefs and standing go-to attitudes. One may find Oneself reflecting on thoughts such as, 'But everything was fine? Why me? What did I do to deserve this?' While the answers to these self-analysis questions will be many and varied, this can be seen as an opportunity to review One's life and One's life journey up until this point in time.

When in this situation, time may feel like it is standing still for One, or even moving backward, as One tries to come to terms with how One is to respond and proceed given this new situation. Whether One's response is a sea-change, tree-change, relationship-change or life-change, it will require time, loving-kindness and support to enable One to embrace any new living outcomes. Be patient with oneself – all of life is a journey towards an inner spiritual path. Remember that all change is a process of inner personal transformation. Create ample space in One's life so that One can reflect, re-evaluate, reorganise, reconfigure and reaffirm a new vision for oneself.

Lao Tzu says:

> Difficult endings often disguise new beginnings.

It is in the space between One's old life and new life that One's mind will find freedom. Freedom to choose to let go of the past, freedom to accept things as they are now and freedom to have faith that 'what will be, will be' in One's life.

With freedom comes choice, and the ability to choose to manifest a living change for oneself. It is also an opportunity to be in a new mind–body space. Have courage and be kind when making any choice and be guided by One's own inner voice and spiritual intuition. Let spirit guide One's way in life – One will be surprised how much will flow to One.

Let One reassure One's mind that it is perfectly okay to be vulnerable and not know the answers to everything. At some points in One's own life, like the ending of One's marriage and the death of One's parents, it was not certain how things would work out for One. But within the life that One has experienced thus far, One has taken time, patience, unconditional love, care, kindness, gentleness and lots of meditation sessions to nurture One's inner wellbeing. There have also been numerous deep and meaningful conversations over tea, drinks and meals with good friends and support from a circle of professionals. One also has unshakeable confidence in oneself, which inspired One to not just survive these experiences but be a better person who will thrive through whatever One encounters in One's life. A belief in One's greater self and an unequivocal trust in the universe that everything will be okay.

There is no greater gift that One can experience than the belief in One's spirit and within oneself in the universe.

There is also no shame in being vulnerable as a human being, either man, woman or transgender. As a quietly spoken man, One acknowledges that One's vulnerability and gentleness is a strength within One's own mind–body and life. Some people may wear their heart on their sleeve, but the true test of a person's inner voice, integrity and authenticity is when One's mind–body is vulnerable and challenged in adverse conditions. This is where the 'real journey' begins to find One's inner path.

An outer journey is only there to precede an inner path.

One's mind is the journey maker, while spirit is the path taker. The truth is that if One has mind, it will create a journey for oneself to follow. This is as true of Buddha as it is of every human being. It is an inescapable truth until One awakens within.

It is like a raindrop falling to the ground. First, it must travel through the air, being blown this way and that, until it finally comes to rest upon the Earth. The flight path of any two raindrops do not occupy the same space and yet they all end up in the same place – on Earth. The raindrops could not have reached the ground any faster than they did, because they had to follow their guided journey, subject to the conditions of their natural course. The same is true of human beings. They also journey along a natural course of events, activities and situations in One's life. The aim is to awaken by mindfully and consciously realising One's inner path before One hits the ground …. or One's mind–body deconstructs and dissolves.

It is never too late to start. One's mind–body is never too young or old to begin. One only needs to open One's mind to embrace the idea of infinite possibilities together with the belief in One's spirit and the intuitive divine knowingness of the universe. All journeys are different, but they all lead to the same inner path within oneself. At some particular point in time, One's story of One's journey becomes irrelevant and will naturally drop away as One becomes more invested in living One's inner path as One's true life. But, up until this time, One will begin to experience an oscillation between One's mind-centredness and spirit-centredness. This is perfectly natural and to be expected.

An egoic mind will insist on being at the centre of decision-making and seek to validate all and everything in One's life. It will resist at every opportunity and use every mental trick in the book to distract, discourage and diminish One's commitment to an inner path. It will require sensory proof and spiritual certainty before it will believe in such an intangible way of living and being.

The good news is that One's spirit knows its true path. There is something incredibly overwhelmingly joyful and beautiful about moving along this inner path – it just feels right and comfortable. It is not something that One can totally explain, but it aligns with an inner sense of spiritual inner peace, mind–body harmony and cosmic balance in One's life. A living cohesion of mind-body-spirit in the now of One's life.

Sometimes One's mind may feel like there is something missing, as if the road ahead needs to be more difficult in order to feel a sense of achievement in One's life, so that it counts for something. This is One's egoic mind's way of justifying effort in One's life. 'Without effort there can be no success' is a modern mantra often recited by motivational professionals to inspire people to keep going, keep achieving and keep striving to attain that outer goal. But it's not the journey in front of One or how long One has travelled along this road that matters, it is the path within oneself. This is what One is really seeking to explore. This is the destination that all divine seekers seek in life. This is the way to One's inner light, eternal peace and spiritual presence. It cannot be traded, bought or sold, it can only be hidden from oneself by One's mind until One realises One's own path and the truth of One's spirit within.

Begin where One is now

It is time to stop running away from oneself, One's family or kinship network, community and Country (land, sea and sky). One needs to turn off all electronic devices and get back to nature and the natural environment. Simply enjoy the sun, moon and stars in the night sky. Take a stroll along the beach, hang out at the beach and listen to the waves, or enjoy a walk along a track in the bush, rainforest or wilderness area. Connect with nature on the simplest level by taking time to be with and talk to a plant, flower, or tree in the garden or recreational park. Observe all that is around One, without identifying, ordering or trying to make sense of it all. Listen to the wind in the trees and the native chorus of birds, bees and bugs. This kind of shared energy is uplifting for One's mind–body–spirit. It is a way to harmonise with the natural order and rhythm of the universe in One's everyday life.

It does not matter how One begins One's journey of enlightenment or spiritual awakening. What matters most is that One simply begins where One is now. One cannot fail at being what One already is – spirit. One can only move forward in a way that either aligns with One's inner Being and is in harmony with the universe or is out of alignment with it all.

Do not be hard on oneself if One is just beginning or does not have a Master, teacher or guide. All the answers will come to One. Have faith and trust that the universe is invested in One's higher self and spiritual success as much as One is too.

Not everything can be learned all at once. The same goes for the creation of this galaxy, solar system and every other celestial object. It is an unfolding and adapting process that is continually self-organising in synchronicity with 'the way' of the universe.

The best way to heal oneself is to simply slow down and take a moment to align with One's inner spirit, soul or cosmic consciousness. One can do this by focusing on One's whole of life wellness and inner wellbeing. Creating space to take loving and good care of One's mind and body is critical to living a prosperous, abundant and long life. Never underestimate the benefits of thinking the 'right thoughts', doing the 'right things' and being in the 'right moment' where One is now. All good things take time and there is always time for good things, good food, good experiences and good people in One's life. Set the intention and then co-create the space. Believe it will come and it will manifest in One's life.

It takes great strength to show kindness, love and compassion to oneself and all – especially Earth. Never let any person persuade One from expressing One's gratitude for these simple quality attributes that reside within oneself.

There is something significant and profound when One realises and begins to enjoy the transcendence to One's own spiritual divinity. Nothing on the face of this Earth comes even close to this.

One's beginning starts with an appreciation and gratitude for all the things that arise out of Country (land, sea and sky) that help nurture and nourish One's human needs (mind and body) in the world. If One looks in a detached way outwards at the world, One will recognise that the universe is truly an abundant place providing all of humankind with the necessary resources to sustain life on planet Earth.

When One stops paying attention to One's outer world and the egoic cravings for ten thousand things and experiences, One can begin to focus on One's inner world and explore the spiritual landscape as an integral part of One's daily life. What else is there out there to attain if One already has enough? Enough water, enough food, enough clothing, enough safety and security, enough love, friends and family, enough health and wellbeing, enough shelter etc. An important question that One needs to ask oneself is, 'When is enough – enough?'

Marcus Aurelius Antoninus was a Roman emperor from 161–180CE and a Stoic philosopher. He was the last of the Five Good Emperors and the last emperor of the Pax Romana (27BCE to 180CE), an age of relative peace and stability for the Roman Empire. Aurelius says:

> Almost nothing material is required for a happy life, for he who has understood existence.

If one has an egoic mind, it will always make a convincing argument or justify the reason that necessary demands or expectations must be met. It will insist that One needs to satisfy an unquenchable thirst for more. The sign of this type of behaviour is when One is mindlessly on autopilot and taking action to grasp for more, challenge more, justify more and try to achieve more in the vain hope that this overthinking and overdoing will somehow fill the void within. What One's egoic mind is really fearful of is loss of control, the silent tranquillity of no-mind, spiritual inner peace and the uncertainty of death.

Egoic thoughts will always complicate One's already complex life even further. One needs to hit the pause button and turn away from this path of inevitable pain. Why give oneself more problems, issues or concerns? The best idea is to simply let go, hit the reset button and begin again. Failure is a necessary part of figuring out the future in the present moment. Never be fearful of beginning again in any aspect of One's life. Everyone makes mistakes and everyone fails at being the person that others expect One to be in this life. So, give oneself a break and let that shit go.

Now is the perfect time to begin – if not then, when? Do not wait for tomorrow or some other day when One thinks it is the right time. The right moment will always be now. Say to oneself, 'Now will always be the right time and right moment to begin.'

One should not focus on how long it will take One to undertake this inner journey of enlightenment and awakening, but the depth to which One surrenders to it within every aspect of One's life. Time has no meaning or value when One is living 'the way' of the path in alignment with life, the universe and everything.

The way is the path

'The way' is an internal path and a fundamental part of being in alignment with One's spirit and the universe. It is experienced as the natural rhythm and intrinsic harmony of living life in cooperation with other sentient Beings on Earth and flowing in synchronicity with the universe itself. Like waves crashing on a beach or a river meandering along towards the sea, it is not attached to anything and yet it has the ability to influence everything it touches. The essence of 'the way' penetrates enlightenment but leaves no trace of ever being attained. None who seek it will find it in the external world, as it resides within the very divine sovereignty of One's infinite existence.

Simplicity is 'the way' itself. It can be expressed in the way One thinks, talks, walks and acts throughout One's life. It is much more than a Zen Buddhist concept of harmony and balance on Country, in the world and on Earth. It exists within the very fabric of space-time and is a principle of the universe's operating system.

If One was to explain this fundamental idea, even the words 'the way' would need to be forgotten to allow One to surrender to it. The more One removes oneself from the sayings, teachings and pointings, the more One is able to experience it within.

The One who holds onto the residue and cannot grasp the real 'isness' of One's infinite existence, distances oneself from the Source or Source Consciousness for all things.

Jalāl ad-Dīn Muhammad Rūmī, more commonly known simply as Rumi, was a 13th century Persian poet, Hanafi faqih, Islamic scholar, Maturidi theologian and Sufi mystic. Rumi says:

As you start to walk on the way, the way appears.

Rumi also says:

The middle path is the way to wisdom.

This is similar to the 'Goldilocks principle' as in the Goldilocks and the Three Bears fairy tale. In this story, a young girl, Goldilocks, becomes lost in the woods and finds the house of the three bears. After entering the dwelling and feeling quite hungry. Goldilocks decides to sample two bowls filled full of porridge on the table. Neither bowl of porridge tasted right – the first bowl was too hot and the second bowl was too cold. Finally, Goldilocks comes across the last bowl, belonging to the baby bear. Goldilocks tastes the contents of this bowl and finds it to be 'not too hot and 'not too cold', but 'just right'.

This story is a good example of how One can and will find One's way in life by allowing things to be as they appear to be. Realise that the 'right path' or 'the way' will eventually be revealed to One at the right moment.

To know the way is to be the way

There are no shortcuts or quick fixes to becoming what One must eventually become in this world – a divine awakened spiritual Being. All things happen for a reason and the reason that something happened is most likely for One's higher self or in the best interests of One's higher purpose. Sometimes things need to fall apart so that One's life can be put back together in a way that aligns with 'the way' of the universe.

When this happens, let it happen and realise that it could not have happened in any other way than how it happened. Accept what is and simply move on with One's life, no matter the significance of the activity, event or circumstances.

Even if One experiences the tragedy of unexpectedly losing a loved one, or some other great calamity in One's life, take some time to reflect mindfully, review soulfully and mourn lovingly the loss. Honour the passing as a gift to Source and simply part of the natural way of the universe. As One moves through the five stages of grief (denial, anger, bargaining, depression and eventually acceptance), One will come to realise that 'the way' of the universe is like an unstoppable cosmic river flowing back to Source. It never begins and it never ends, as it is all part of the continuum of beingness, which is integral to One's infinite existence and the universe itself.

Believe it or not, One has the intuitive intelligence to live a life that simply aligns with 'the way'. One is capable of opening One's mind and seeing things in a new light. One can progressively train One's mind to be positive and aligned and recognise when One is flowing with 'the way'. This will appear as a stream of mindful effortlessness when One is being truly and fully present in One's life. It will not remove difficult challenges, complex problems or stubborn obstacles in One's path, because effort and action will still be required to move beyond that which One is faced with in life.

Lao Tzu says:

> The way to do is to be.

This is a very profound statement when referring to how to consider 'the way'. It is a good summary of Tzu's teachings and living principles of what to do by simply being in the moment of One's life now.

When things become too much in One's life and the pressure of living is overwhelming, take a moment to stop, pause and ponder. Recognise that this pain in One's life is a sign from the universe. Learn to read the signals that something is not quite right and that One needs to make a course correction in this moment and to whatever One is doing today. Become aware that One is not aligned with 'the way'.

One may not know exactly where One needs to be in One's life, but this is okay. Simply do the best that One can with whatever One has. Invite friends, family and the universe to help One. One may be surprised by who answers the call. Do not try and control the outcome of the situation. Instead, focus on accepting, adjusting and adapting to where One is now. Let everything then flow from this point forward.

Stop trying to prove oneself to others or meet people's expectations. Make a conscious decision to simply flow with 'the way'. One is not responsible for the versions of oneself that exist in other people's minds, be it good or bad. What others see in One is a reflection of these minds. If another sees oneself in a particular way, it is because this person looks at oneself with this filter in mind. Stand tall and be proud that One is following One's own inner path along 'the way' to where One is now. Once One realises that One is worthy, One is whole and One is capable of being the best version of oneself, One will never need to compare oneself with any other person on the planet.

'The way' is not a path to accumulate more material things, exciting experiences or personal pleasures effortlessly. It is a spiritual path where One gives things away. One is more likely to give away attachment to thoughts and things, judgement of others and objects, and resistance to people's differing perspectives and change.

When One is aligned to One's divine mission and purpose to become an awakened sentient Being of the universe, One creates an inner life of aligned joy, peace and oneness on Earth.

Simple spiritual living

One must ask oneself this question, 'How does One live a simple spiritual life?' A life free of endless debt, ongoing stress and painful anxiety about the future. The answer lies in being grateful, joyful and content with what One has and not wasting One's energy or focusing on what One does not. Whatever One's thoughts are aligned to at this moment is exactly the message that One is vibrating into the universe. The Law of Attraction suggests that One's vibrations attract everything that One is attuned to at that particular vibrating frequency. Being loving attracts love, being prosperous and abundant attracts prosperity and abundance, and being joyful attracts more joy in One's life. It is that simple and uncomplicated.

Know that the universe is always on. It is continually receiving, listening and responding to One's mind–body–spirit vibrations. The universe only reflects and gives One more of the same. If One is joyfully happy or positively optimistic about life, this will be reflected back to One like a mirror or be manifested in One's life. This is also true for those who choose to be angry, hateful, selfish, deceitful, violent, hurtful or negative. The universe will harmonise and reflect those vibrations back to these individuals. The universe or Source only gives One that which One is willing to align to at this moment now.

Be as excited as a child about whatever may unfold or manifest in One's life. Carl Jung says:

> That which we do not bring to consciousness appears in our lives as fate.

As a creator of One's reality, become fully awake to oneself.

To experience something different in One's life, One must consciously choose to believe differently, think differently, act or speak differently, react or behave differently and live differently.

To live simply, One must believe in simplicity as a way of living life. The first step along 'the way' is to make space in One's life for being simple and spiritual. This does not mean giving away all of One's current material possessions or shaving One's head. It is about recognising and making One's life a sacred space for living a simple spiritual life. It is making a commitment to oneself about being in alignment with living on Country, Earth and in the universe. Lao Tzu says:

> When you succeed in connecting your energy with the divine realm through high awareness and the practice of undiscriminating virtue, the transmission of the ultimate subtle truths will follow.

Give oneself permission to walk away, leave a situation or remove oneself from a relationship that is vibrating at a negative frequency. There is no need to explain it or make sense of it. If its vibe is out of alignment with One's sense of wellbeing, ensure that One honours oneself by being in a different place and space. Trust One's inner voice and intuition to inform One's higher self and decision-making process in One's life.

When One chooses to let go of egoic-based thinking and behaviours, such as the need to be right, social validation of One's human identity or divisiveness and control over people, One creates more space in One's life to just be. One is more than One's mind–body or One's collective memory, constructed personhood, social role, academic achievements, conditioned thinking or limited experiences in the world.

When One speaks what One seeks, One opens up a divine dialogue with the universe about where One desires to be in life. Speaking about One's vision and writing it down is a way to create neural pathways in the brain that affirm this new reality. Allow oneself to believe in this new reality as if it already exists now. A simple spiritual life, mindfully aligned to One's spirit and flowing with 'the way' of the universe. Imagine what it looks like, sounds like, feels like, tastes like and smells like.

Lao Tzu says:

> To realise the constancy and steadiness in your life is to realise the deep nature of the universe. This realisation is not dependent on any transitory internal or external condition, rather it is an expression of one's own immutable spiritual nature. The only way to attain the Universal Way is to maintain the integral virtues of the constancy, steadiness and simplicity in one's daily life.

Let no person distract oneself from this goal in life. Stop waiting for others to endorse, affirm or validate a change in One's life. It is up to One to motivate, encourage and inspire oneself along this journey. Make no particular plans other than to commit oneself along 'the way' to living a simple spiritual life.

This new life will probably require the removal of unhealthy products, harmful practices and toxic people from One's circle of life. Do not feel surprised or guilty if some of One's previous friends and family begin to fade away or withdraw from One's friendship circle. It is only natural that One will experience a certain level of isolation when living an awakened lifestyle in an insane world.

When One finally begins to 'wake up' and realise that One has been living in a dream world, One's initial reaction will most likely be profound amazement or overwhelming excitement, followed by shock and a deep sense of self-reflection that One has been asleep for decades.

Do not be surprised that at the innermost core of One's Being there is an incredible deep longing to simply just be. One's Being desires to affirm its inner essence on Earth as spirit and live a spiritual life.

With every breath, commit One's mind, body and spirit to living from the heart of One's spiritual existence. Be a witness to One's actions to live virtuously throughout the day and over the course of One's lifetime. Realise that spirit has no timeline and the universe has no agenda.

Share and improve the lives of others by first dedicating oneself to improving One's own life.

Spiritual rules for living

Lao Tzu created four cardinal rules, virtues or principles of living. Lao Tzu believed that living a life centred around these rules would allow one to access true wisdom from the universe and align oneself with the Source, the Creator, Great Spirit, God, Allah or the Supreme Being.

Lao Tzu's spiritual rules for living include:

1. Reverence for all life

This rule is about how One should respect all life. It is a recognition that One's human existence depends on all other life on the planet. One must love and honour oneself and thus treat all with respect, kindness, and gratitude. Lao Tzu believed everyone can live in peace and harmony if One remembers this first spiritual rule of living.

2. Natural sincerity

The second rule is about being honest, simple and authentic. It is learning to live One's life from the centrepoint of One's own spiritual truth and not being swayed by ego-centric minds. It is realising One's true nature as a sentient Being of the universe and knowing that, when One does this, everything else will fall into place as effortlessly as the sun shining or the Earth spinning on its axis. This kind of living inspires others to do the same and be true to One's inner spirit. When One allows oneself to align in natural harmony with One's authentic self, One's thoughts and actions become meaningful and sincere in this world.

3. Gentleness

The third rule is focused on living life with grace and gentleness as One goes about One's daily tasks. It is also about being loving, kind and compassionate. No matter what One encounters in One's day or in One's life, respond with kindness and gentleness. Do not react to egoic thinking or behaviours of others. Simply practice gentleness in how One thinks, speaks and acts. Gentleness, love and kindness is a strength, not a weakness. When One practices gentleness, One awakens oneself and the world to what truly matters in life.

4. Supportiveness

The fourth rule is about supporting oneself so that One is able to support others on One's life quest and spiritual journey. One can only give what One has to offer. To live a life of service is a noble virtue and a life that honours the impermanence of life itself. When One serves all, everyone benefits on Earth. The simple act of serving another human being is in itself a gift of loving-kindness from a generous spirit. When One lives to pay it forward, this creates a reality of prosperity and abundance that benefits all sentient Beings living in this world. One's joy will always be found in helping others without expectation.

Dr Wayne Dyer says:

> The greatest joy comes from giving and serving, so replace your habit of focusing exclusively on yourself and what's in it for you. When you make the shift to supporting others in your life, without expecting anything in return, you'll think less about what you want and find comfort and joy in the act of giving and serving.

Learning to imbue One's life with these virtues or principles for life will create an experience of living with grace and ease on a daily basis. Each rule brings a sense of lightness, gracefulness and easy-going flow to living a spiritual life. It also helps in letting go of self-limiting negative beliefs, harmful life patterns and unhealthy addictions that tend to adversely impact One's inner peace, joy and oneness.

Dr Wayne Dyer also says:

> The four cardinal virtues are a road map to the simple truth of the universe. To revere all of life, to live with natural sincerity, to practice gentleness, and to be in service to others is to replicate the energy field from which you originated.

Collective wellness and individual wellbeing

Mental wellness, physical wellness and spiritual wellness are all interrelated and interconnected in the universe. All influence each other in a variety of different ways in the world. What the mind perceives as real, the body reacts to, and vice versa. Mind and body are so interrelated that it is sometimes hard to separate one from the other. This suggests that, when responding to unwellness within oneself, One should treat both to gain the most benefit for a healthy life and affirm One's positive wellbeing.

The World Health Organization (WHO) says:

> Health is a state of complete physical, mental and social well-being and not merely the absence of disease and infirmity.

There is a growing consensus of opinions within health care and wellness professionals who are now promoting the idea that between 40% and 60% of all illnesses or unwellness can be treated and cured by simply having a positive mindset and optimistic outlook about One's personal wellbeing. This is amazing and astounding, to say the least. It means that One can think or program oneself to be well and know that it will work in most cases. It also means at the extreme end of the spectrum of life that if One is experiencing a critical injury and One believes One's mind-body is going to die – One will. On the other hand, if One's mind-body believes that One is going to survive and live – One will. Whatever One believes, One will be right.

Lavleen Kaur, an award-winning dietitian, clinical nutritionist and lifestyle coach from Chandigarh, India has suggested that up to 95% of all chronic disease is caused by One's food choices, toxic food ingredients, nutritional deficiencies and a lack of physical exercise. No amount of wishing illness or pain away will result in a better life. One needs to be an active participant in One's own living wellness and personal wellbeing. One must embrace a positive mind, a positive vibe and a positive lifestyle. It is too important to be outsourced to another person.

The best thing One can ever do is believe in oneself. Reimagine oneself and who One thinks One is now. Be thankful for the mind, body and spirit that already exists. Being well is an inside job – begin there. Buddha says:

> To keep the body in good health is a duty, otherwise we shall not be able to keep our mind strong and clear.

Taking care of others should not be done at the expense of oneself. Fill and replenish One's own individual well of mental, physical and spiritual wellness first, and as many times as necessary. One can only give to others what One has. When One looks after oneself, One is in a better position to look after others, Country, the world and Earth. To heal others, Country and the Earth, One must first heal oneself. This is not a selfish act, it is a kind, loving and compassionate action towards oneself. Buddha says:

> You, yourself, as much as anybody in the entire universe, deserve your love and affection.

The practice of mindfulness in One's daily life is essential for bringing One in alignment with One's spirit, being on Country and in the universe. The benefits of mindfulness practices include a range of mental benefits, physical benefits and spiritual benefits. These include but are not limited to the following.

Mental benefits:
- Decreases stress, worry and anxiety within One's mind
- Improves One's overall mental clarity and calmness
- Better management of One's thoughts, impulse control etc
- Improves One's learning and academic results
- Helps with depression and addiction that One may be experiencing
- Promotes better communication and interpersonal relationships with others

Physical benefits:
- Improves One's sleep
- Boosts One's energy levels
- Promotes higher serotonin levels in One's brain
- Helps One's weight loss and food consumption/ management
- Better general wellness and inner health within oneself
- Promotes a feeling and sense of overall calm, safety and security within oneself

Spiritual benefits:
- Improves alignment with One's spirit, living on Country and the universe
- Increases One's inner awareness and intuitive intelligence
- Promotes a greater oneness within oneself and with all
- Creates a higher harmonic resonance with all sentient Beings in the universe

- Increases One's realisation of One's path of enlightenment
- Enables One's inner awakening to One's divine truth and sense of divinity

Illness or unwellness is expensive, which is why a small amount of investment in One's wellness every day is important. The Dalai Lama says:

Happiness is the highest form of health.

This is why One's inner joy is so important, as well as having the ability to laugh at oneself for no particular reason. One is drawn to the common phrase, 'laughter is good medicine', and it is true.

Keeping or maintaining One's sanity in a world that seems to be run by egocentric people who value greed over gratitude, control over compassion, separation over sanity and judgement over inner joy can be a full-time job. There are many examples where millions of individual minds and global companies are putting profits over people and the planet in the pursuit of fulfilling an egoic desire – more money. However, this is changing and with the awakening of more conscious Beings on Earth, the process of spiritual evolution will increase exponentially in the coming years and decades.

The best way to support the evolution of spiritual Beings on the planet is to focus individually and collectively on the six domains of wellness:

1. Mental
2. Physical
3. Spiritual
4. Social and emotional
5. Family and community
6. Cultural

It is no surprise that these six domains are interconnected and interrelated. The wellness of any person, place or planet needs to take into consideration all these domains collectively, not just respond to or treat in isolation.

If One is to attract and experience a better life, lifestyle and whole of life wellness, One needs to become a better version of oneself. Better at looking after and supporting all six domains of wellness in One's life. One cannot do the same things that One has always done and expect change to simply just magically happen or One's life to surprisingly improve. It should not be a painful process, but it may be experienced as part of One's personal mental, physical and spiritual growth moments.

One cannot blame anyone or anything for how One's life is now. It is what it is, and One needs to accept it and move on graciously and with humility. It is time to take full responsibility for One's mind–body–spirit and reality.

Begin by training One's mind in the way of meditation and mindfulness practices. Create space in One's life to deeply look within One's spirit and align with Country and the universe. Transform One's living habits a day at a time. Start upgrading One's living virtues or life principles to be spiritually centred, joyfully present and openly optimistic as well as unconditionally positive.

Let One's spiritual principle and vibe for this year be to let go of unhealthy thoughts and habits, toxic relationships and friends, negative life patterns and behaviours, and unnatural and harmful attachments. It is time to flip the script on One's old ways and embrace new ways that promote, enhance and increase One's participation in expanding One's collective wellness and personal wellbeing.

Mental wellness

Creating mental wellness in One's life is not just about the reduction, removal or absence of negative thoughts in One's mind. It is about how One promotes and continually improves individual memes within One's psychological landscape.

This means using One's thinking to enable and support One's cognitive and emotional capabilities to effectively and mindfully function in society so One can meet the ordinary demands of everyday life. Being well within One's mind is learning how to let go of everything that does not serve One today or in this moment. In meditation, One learns that using this practice is not to attain anything or a particular state of mind, but to remove all obstacles or mental blocks to free oneself. Then One is free to realise One's path of enlightenment and be awake now.

Physical wellness

There are five key aspects of physical wellness: sleep, eating well, physical activity, hygiene and relaxation. Physical wellness is about getting adequate sleep each day, eating a healthy and balanced diet (plus additional vitamin supplements or prescribed medications if needed), being physically active every day and looking after One's body, including getting an annual medical check, and learning to rest, relax, release muscle tension and refresh One's body. Create space to enjoy a regular therapeutic massage or other relaxing and soothing treatment, like a warm bath. To invest in One's physical wellness by undertaking simple health maintenance activities, like daily practices of showering, washing hands, brushing teeth and drinking plenty of water, is to set oneself up for a long and prosperous life on Earth.

Spiritual wellness

Spiritual wellness is about learning to listen to One's intuitive intelligence and aligning with One's spirit and the universe. It is recognising that spirit, soul or cosmic consciousness is imbued with seven states of spiritual consciousness: knowing, awareness, oneness, joy, free will, peace and presence. Spiritual wellness is about being centred within and operating from a paradigm of living life as a divine sentient Being of the universe. This means going about One's daily activities and being mindful that One is spirit hosting a human form on Earth. One exists within a continuum of beingness which is all part of One's infinite existence in the universe. One's spirit cannot die because One was never born. One's spirit is and has always been immortal, eternal and infinite.

Social and emotional wellness

Social and emotional wellness is essential for One's overall health and wellbeing. Being socially and emotionally well means being able to realise One's abilities, cope with the normal stresses of everyday life, engage and work productively, and contribute to One's community in a positive way. Positive effects of social and emotional wellness are reflected in One's feelings or a sense of psychological safeness, safety, secureness or security in One's personal life, relationships with a partner, friends and family as well as at work. A combination of being a healthy individual and experiencing healthy places living on Country and in the world are most effective in promoting social and emotional wellness in One's life.

Family and community wellness

Family and community wellness is about creating and maintaining strong, flexible and adaptable partnerships between family members and with individuals in the community in which One lives. It is built on shared values, mutual respect, common vision and emphasises the strengths, skills and quality attributes that all stakeholders bring to the relationship or collective experience as it changes over time. Family and community wellness enables a healthy and supportive space for open communication, which promotes trust and respect between all participants. This in turn helps to cultivate a sense of belonging among individual family and community members, which also creates caring, loving and nurturing experiences that benefit the next generation.

Cultural wellness

Cultural wellness is about working, living and being on Country (land, sea and sky). It is also about being aware of One's own cultural beliefs, practices, habits or behaviours and how One interacts with others who are different from oneself in terms of Country (land, sea and sky), ethnicity, religion, gender, sexual orientation, age or customs (practices). It is about developing and maintaining healthy relationships, accepting and understanding other ways of living and being, and supporting diversity on Country, in the world and universe. This involves having the quiet confidence to positively interact with others in the world or around One, using good communication skills, open and friendly living practices, respecting oneself and others, as well as creating a support system and safe space for mutual exchange, information sharing and cultural benefits.

Going with the flow of life

When One is in alignment with One's spirit, Country and the universe, simply allow all things to just be and flow naturally forward with ease and effortlessness. One will know that One's mind–body–spirit is in this state when One feels and experiences a non-resistance and harmonic synchronicity with all life around One. One will begin to notice that One's spiritual presence is fully engaged and yet One's mind–body is quietly detached at the same time. This does not mean that One does not care about the people, place or planet on which One lives. It is simply a reflection of where One is now.

Resist trying to change the flow of life. Simply be an observer of it like the sky watching a majestic river flow out to sea. Lao Tzu says:

> Life is a series of natural and spontaneous changes. Don't resist them; that only creates sorrow. Let reality be reality. Let things flow naturally forward in whatever way they like.

When One wakes in the morning, remind oneself to be fully present and to flow with life. Whatever is going to happen today will happen – accept it in the moment. One is not responsible for the thoughts and actions of other minds on Earth. Focus on using One's time on Earth to be mindfully and spiritually centred first. Then consciously move forward in the direction of One's choosing.

Modern work-life has a way of appearing to be on 24 hours a day and seven days a week. It is very easy to get caught up in the modern lifecycle of 'eat-work-sleep-repeat'. There seems to be no time for anything else. However, this is not true. One can break this egoic pattern of behaviours by introducing a range of new habits and perspectives simply by consciously choosing to, in alignment with One's spirit and act virtuously in every aspect of One's daily life. It is not as hard as it seems. Give it a go and move One's mind to a place of acceptance to free One's life so One will be forever free now.

Plan to unplan One's life and everything in it. This may seem like a contradiction, but it is not. Sometimes the best thing that One can do in life is not plan and just allow oneself to be in the moment. One has often found the most rewarding outcomes in life have been as a result of letting go and flowing with whatever was happening.

Do not be pressured by external expectations to 'get things done' out of fear that someone will be disappointed in oneself. Simply do the best that One can. If necessary, ask others for help and assistance. All life is a shared responsibility and living experience. Invite the universe to guide One on One's way in life. Let things flow in a way that aligns with One's inner peace of mind and spirit. One is not here to accomplish thousands of things in life. Simplicity and balance are the keys to a great life. Focus on one simple thing at a time. Do it mindfully, effortlessly, gently, lovingly and with a spiritual sense of cosmic calm. Buddha says:

> In the end, only three things matter: how much you loved, how gently you lived, and how gracefully you let go of things not meant for you.

The way to go with the flow is to first realise when One is not flowing with the natural rhythm of life. This means that One needs to become aware of One's thoughts, behaviours and actions.

One needs to ask oneself these questions: Is One rushing about in One's life? Is One going from task to task, activity or event in One's daily life without taking a break or pausing in between? Does One think that One needs to be continually achieving in order to get somewhere in life rather than just allowing oneself to be in the moment? Does One believe that One needs to keep mentally active in One's mind or busy in One's daily life because One is fearful of what may happen or that others may think poorly of oneself?

If One answered 'yes' to any of these questions, it means that One is not flowing with 'the way' of the universe. Know that the universe will not give oneself cosmic karmic credits for the things One achieves in life. It will simply reflect the same vibrational energy that One chooses to activate and radiate out into the world.

One must realise that what breaks was meant to be broken, what did not happen was not meant to happen, and whoever One did not meet was never meant to be met. This is not about looking at the universe from a deficit model but being aware of how the universe works in favour of One's higher self and divine consciousness. One should free oneself of One's past because One will only ever exist in the present.

Many people find it difficult to let go and go with the flow of life. Not because it is a complicated concept or task, but because most people choose and prefer a form of suffering that they are intimately familiar with. This attachment to One's suffering makes it appears as if it was always meant to be. The truth is, this is a false construct formed out of a particular behaviour that has probably become an ingrained habit or living practice in One's life. Stepping into the unknown raises many fears and doubts within One's mind. It feeds ego-centric negative thought patterns, memes of self-doubt and feelings of unworthiness.

As the day surrenders to the night, One must surrender One's suffering to 'the way'. Eckhart Tolle says:

> To some people, surrender may have negative connotations, implying defeat, giving up, failing to rise to the challenges of life, becoming lethargic and so on. True surrender, however, is something entirely different. It does not mean to passively put up with whatever situation you find yourself in and to do nothing about it. Nor does it mean to cease making plans or initiating positive action. Surrender is the simple but profound wisdom to yielding rather than opposing the flow of life.

The more One tries to control life and its outcome, the more one will repeatedly fail in the process of living life itself. Know that what binds the universe together is within all things. It permeates the very air that One breathes and everything on Country (land, sea and sky). First Nations peoples have understood and known about this invisible connection with all living things. It has always been a part of creation since the beginning. It exists in all the elements on Earth and in the very fabric of One's human form. One cannot outrun it, hide from it or escape it. One can only honour it and give One's thanks and gratitude for being in this moment as One experiences the life One has on Earth.

An important realisation to flowing with 'the way' of the universe is knowing that One is already part of a great cosmic journey, making its way back to Source or the divine light of infinite existence. Do not fight it or try to escape it, simply let go and move in harmony with the natural current of life. The more One struggles, the more One will endure pain and suffering. The more One is able to embrace the truth of One's infinite existence, the more One will be able to experience a ribbon of light, love and oneness flowing through One's life.

An egoic mind will always ask more of oneself before it surrenders 'control' – more intellectual understanding, more evidence and more proof. Nothing will ever be good enough for a mind that is preconditioned with egoic thoughts. It will never think it is worthy enough, good enough or precious enough to be of value in One's life or this world. This is why One must remove One's locus of control from being mind-centred to spirit-centred. This is all part of the process of self-realisation and awakening. To a mind that is calm, quiet and free, the universe shall reveal all to One's spirit.

Lao Tzu says:

> Those who flow as life flows knows that they need no other force.

Living One's inner way now

Suggestions for putting the learnings, teachings and pointings of this chapter into practice in One's daily life:

- Know that One is exactly where One needs to be at this moment in One's life now.
- Allow One's life to flow simply, naturally and effortlessly along 'the way' of the universe.
- Be open to everything and attached to nothing as One achieves and goes about One's daily tasks or life. Simply let life be life. Ride the wave of life with ease and effortlessness.
- Engage with all sentient Beings with grace, gentleness and humility.
- That which is meant for One will come to One in the right time and the right way. Trust the process and the universe that everything and everyone will arrive on time.
- Flow with life and in synchronicity with the universe itself.

CHAPTER 4

Co-existence
Manifesting Conscious Experiences

Origin of One's existence

One's human form exists because of thousands of years of love and an uninterrupted lineage of cosmic spiritual connections. Sentient visitors who found each other on this habitable blue-green planet in a distant part of the known universe, after aligning in harmony through a force of universal synergy, decided to share One's unconditional divine love with One another. For a brief moment in time, two spiritual Beings chose to affirm One's light, love and oneness for each other in the world and on Earth.

One is not here by random chance, One is here by divine choice. It is no accident that One is exactly where One is now, doing what must be done or undone in the world. One's inner free will brought One to this planet, this time and this moment now. Not some random act or future fate of the universe at work. Know that there are no coincidences in the universe, just 'the way' of life that One is intrinsically part of in this world. As a spiritual sentient Being, One originates from Source or Source Consciousness. It is the cosmic or divine light of the universe existing within a continuum of unending beingness. One's infinite existence in this world requires no proof to others as it is not a tangible object, but a collective state of existence in the universe. One is imbued with these states of existence and in essence One's spiritual identity. These seven states are knowing, awareness, oneness, joy, free will, peace and presence.

One's spirit exists beyond the tangible reality of One's three-dimensional, human-based construct or DNA avatar. It is not something that One can point to, touch or take hold of in a physical sense. But it is real, nonetheless. It is a cosmic reality that is very real, very knowable and very much 'alive' as One's spiritual presence in the world.

One's human form is created out of stardust. One is integral to the planet and its place in the universe. Every part of One's human form was once part of something else on Earth. This is why One is able to state that One is made from the water in the clouds above, the earth beneath One's feet and all living things in this world. Know that One's body is now composed of completely different molecules and atoms than it was on the day of One's birth. Swedish molecular biologist Dr Jonas Frisen found that One's body largely replaces and renews its biological structure every seven to ten years. The human body is continually in flux, whether it is growing new hairs, shedding its skin or renewing its lungs. How can One ever say that One's form or oneself is the same living person as when One's human form was created.

One's mind–body is continually in a process of renewal and reconfiguration of itself. Without this, One's form would be unable to grow, be flexible and continually adapt to all the external and internal changes in One's life. The universe or altered consciousness works in a similar way – ever changing, continually evolving and perpetually reconfiguring all things within it.

Charles Darwin was an English naturalist, geologist and biologist, best known for his significant contributions to the science of evolution. His proposal that all species of life have descended from common ancestors is now widely accepted and considered as a fundamental concept. Darwin published his theory of evolution in 1859 with compelling evidence in his book On the Origin of Species. Charles Darwin says:

> It is not the most intellectual of the species that survives; it is not the strongest that survives; but the species that survives is the one that is able best to adapt and adjust to the changing environment in which it finds itself.

In a world full of mindless egoic chatter and social media commenting on who One should become and how One needs to think and behave, it is time to stop for a moment and listen to the truth within oneself. Imagine that One did not have any expectations thrust upon One. One could simply be and do One's best in life. What if One was free of external and internal criticism? What if whatever One did today was enough and tomorrow was another day? What if One could be immensely proud of oneself for simply existing and being on Earth? One can and should. One's spirit is not subject to the expectations of other human beings. One need not accept criticisms or complaints for being a sentient Being and doing the best with One's human form, thoughts and behaviours.

One will come into contact with a lot of people on the planet who are operating at a lower level of consciousness. Simply meet people where everyone is and not where One wants others to be. It is not One's job to point out the lower vibrating frequency of those that One meets on a daily basis. Everyone's spiritual journey is different, but all follow the same path in life, returning to Source. One merely needs to respond virtuously with kindness, gentleness and compassion in every situation no matter the circumstances One finds oneself in at the time. Knowing One's spiritual origins in the universe is a shield of light. It cannot be removed or tarnished, no matter what One encounters or faces in this life. One has an indomitable spirit with limitless potential.

One's human form was created out of the ashes of other stars and cosmic dust of disintegrated planets in this galaxy. Lift One's head and raise One's level of thinking to vibrate at a higher level of cosmic consciousness now.

One comes to this planet imbued with pure divine cosmic consciousness. What flows within and emanates from One's spirit is the same as the divinity of creation or Allah, God, the Creator. How can One think less of oneself if One originates from the Source of all things in the universe?

One is, and has always been, nameless, sexless, egoless, formless, raceless, nationless, fearless, boundless, cultureless, dimensionless, limitless and timeless. In every way imaginable, One is truly an incredible immeasurable and powerful sentient Being of the universe. Believe – so be it now.

When One has the courage to choose a different starting point for One's life on Earth, guess what happens? The whole trajectory of One's life and living experiences on the planet changes. It is that simple. This is not a trick of the universe. It is about starting One's life from a different spiritual space and mindful place. It is realising that One does not need to play the game of ego and 'fit in' to the existing mindscape of egoic agendas of others on the planet. Although 99% of the people in One's life will most likely believe One has gone insane, take comfort in walking One's own inner path of personal prosperity and awakened abundance in this world. Initiate action to reset, reimagine and realign One's life compass so that it points inwards to One's true spiritual direction in life.

Richard L. Evans, best known for his inspirational messages, says:

Your direction is more important than your speed.

This is important to remember when moving forward in One's life. However, what precedes this thought is that intention is more important than direction.

Knowing where One comes from is as important as knowing where One is going in the world and the universe. It is easy to get lost in a world with so much mixed messaging. This is why mindfulness and meditation offer One a way to align with One's spirit. Daily meditation practices help One figure out One's inner mindscape and spiritual space in the world. Wherever One is, One is home in the universe.

Be aware that every sentient Being who has ever arrived on Earth comes from the same state of unending beingness as One. One's origin is from an infinite state of cosmic existence and not from an alternative multi or parallel universe or fifth dimension. The intuitive intelligence of most spiritual Beings is suppressed and overridden by the constructed social programming of the culture in which One is raised in the world. Most social groups and human cultures ignore this spiritual beginning. This is why humans become mind-centred and move along their spiritual journey with a conditioned and egoic mind through the childhood and formative years. Countless people over the millennium have been taught from generation to generation not to believe in the origins of One's divine existence. However, spirit and One's connection to the universe are widely known by First Nations. It has been an integral part of First Nations peoples' living beliefs, social habits and cultural practices.

If the divine truth and origin of One's existence was affirmed and acknowledged from the beginning of One's life or birth, it would completely change the face of Earth. It would become an interstellar, spiritually based, Type 1 civilisation in the galaxy. Everyone would realise from the start of One's life that One is a divine sentient Being of the universe. Knowing this would create unity, improve harmony and establish universal common ground between all peoples. The sooner humanity becomes aware of One's infinite existence, the sooner all of humankind will spiritually evolve.

Creating space for new relationships

The first and most important relationship One will ever have in life is with oneself. How One sees or perceives oneself, how One talks to oneself, how One treats oneself and how One heals oneself is critically important in determining One's living experiences and life on Earth. One's life is as significant as everyone else's life in the world. Take the time to be well, love well and live well as much as One possibly can over the course of One's life. Do not make the mistake of rushing through life onto the next exciting thing. Destination addiction is a sign that One's mind is being driven by egoic thoughts of inadequacy and restlessness. Nothing and no person will ever be good enough for an egoic mind, as it will always seek to move beyond the present to the past or the future in the hope of attaining something better. Relationships between people often fail because one or both minds are operating from a self-serving, egoic framework. The most tangible sign of an egoic mind is that One will always be concerned with the idea or question 'What's in it for me?' A mind operating from a spirit-centred perspective will often embrace or ask the question 'How may One be of service or help?' This is the difference. Egoic-type people tend to help oneself, whereas spirit-type people tend to help or serve others.

If One ever believes that One should be with another spiritual Being or in a different relationship, be aware that anything can happen and sometimes it does. Know that all things will come to One as surely as the tide comes in and the sun rises in the morning sky.

Have faith that One is where One needs to be at this moment in time and One is with the right person as well. Even if One is single, this is the right space and place for One now. Just because One is alone does not mean that One is automatically lonely. Feeling alone is an emotional response to an idea or the thought of being by oneself. Know that One is not alone in the universe. One's silent partner in all things in life is the universe itself.

Learning to create space in One's life is the first step in manifesting new experiences and relationships. Once One becomes aware of this, One can take mindful action to change any or all aspects of One's life. It is difficult to share new experiences, explore new places or meet new people if One's life is full to the brim and jam-packed with an overflowing schedule of rolling activities and events. Being busy all the time is not an excuse that One can use in order to avoid creating space. One must take complete responsibility for One's spiritual life and loving relationships. Just because things did not work out in the past does not mean that One is destined to relive or experience the same outcome. One needs to hit the reset button and begin again. Painful endings or dissolved relationships often lead to increased awareness, life learnings and new beginnings. Do not underestimate the ability of oneself or the universe to bring about positive change within One's life on Earth.

One of the greatest assets that One will ever have or experience in life is open space or the emptiness of nothingness. Space in One's mind to think, space in One's lungs to breathe, space in One's life to live and living space to simply be in the moment. Space is often seen as a useless void or empty nothingness. One will hear others say, 'There is nothing there, nobody around and nothing to do'. These are exactly the reasons that make space so valuable, precious and significant in One's life.

Albert Einstein says:

Time and space are not conditions of existence, time and space is a model of thinking.

When One changes the way that One views or looks at space, something wonderful begins to happen within oneself and in One's life. One begins to see that One exists in a unified field of infinite potential where anything is possible.

Buddha says:

> All that we are is the result of what we have thought. The mind is everything. What we think we become.

The more One values space, the more One becomes aware of the infinite possibilities in which One's life may flow and how it may unfold. One begins to realise that One is not stuck where One is, One is simply on the cusp of something new, something wonderful or something magical. One's divine destiny is not fixed in time or space, nor is One bound by them. With space as One's starting point in life, One can imagine new possibilities, new opportunities, new experiences and new relationships.

Thich Nhat Hanh says:

Thanks to impermanence, everything is possible.

The way to co-create better relationships with oneself, living on Country, other people and the universe is to give oneself the gift of space.

It is important to realise that all relationships are impermanent. Eventually, every person will die and leave One's life. It is an inevitability that One will experience.

Buddha says:

The world is in continuous flux and is impermanent.

Knowing that nothing is permanent in this world, One will realise that all conditioned thinking and things in life will always change. If One desires space, then rather than saying 'I want space', say 'One chooses space', or 'One chooses love, freedom, prosperity or abundance now'. When One does this, One is making a conscious choice to alter One's living reality and affirm a different reality in the universe. One is mindfully and consciously aligning to an alternate future at this moment.

If One says 'I want' this or that thing, person or experience, One is affirming a deficit or lacking perspective. One is creating thought stream or vibrational messaging to the universe that One is living a life that is less than, is lacking in some way or is a non-abundant state of existence. One is stuck in limbo, perpetually seeking something. This is like looking at the world with a glass half-empty rather than a glass half-full. Know that the universe will only respond to One's vibrational vision or new manifested reality as One sees it. Affirm a future out of love, not lack.

This is why One will hear people falling into the trap of saying or asking 'Why can't I have this?' or 'Why can't I have what I want?' These statements are classic examples of asking for things that will never arrive. One needs to flip the script on this kind of statement. One does this by changing it from a fear-based question to a statement of 'aligned destiny', which attracts a new vibrational experience or manifests a new reality.

When One stops seeking out of fear, One is able to attract with an alignment of being. Train One's mind to respond to hurt, pain and fear with kindness, gentleness, compassion and openness. No matter what One has experienced in One's life or relationships, make a conscious commitment to oneself to be open. Open to anything. Open to change. Open to listening without judging, commenting or analysing. Open to innovative ideas and suggestions. Open to healing One's mind–body. Open to new possibilities, friendships and relationships. Open to space for the unknown in One's life.

Know that the universe is on One's side and acts in the best interests of One's higher self.

When One says 'One chooses space for love or to be love or to be loving', One is sending a cosmic vibration into the universe to manifest an alternate reality that aligns with the intention for this space. The universe will naturally attune to this vibration and harmonise with it. This is why space is so powerful in One's life. Space precedes all that One chooses to manifest in this world. Space in and of itself has no fear, no doubt and nothing to cling to. It is just free to hold whatever is needed to be held. This is why all illusions are able to exist within altered consciousness or the universe. Space is free. Space is omnipresent. Space exists even when it appears not to be available.

When One chooses space, One is choosing freedom. Freedom to change and co-create the best version of oneself, freedom to manifest One's aligned destiny and freedom to be present in this moment.

Unconditional love, inner peace and spiritual service

To choose unconditional love, inner peace and living in service over everything else in One's life is a significant sign of inner alignment with One's Being in the universe. Let nothing and no person in this world stop One from living life on One's own spiritual terms and in One's own mindful way. Within One is all the answers. One knows who One is. In addition, One is aware of what path to journey along in order to reach One's full potential and achieve One's divine purpose.

Make a conscious decision to choose to be loving, kind and compassionate. Then watch how One's path in life unfolds in this way. It is only after One makes a conscious choice that the universe can respond more appropriately and effectively in the moment of One's choosing. Choosing to be virtuous in every aspect of One's life is a great and humble way to live on the planet. One brings loving, kind energy and spiritual awareness to this day and to One's life. One knows that One deserves the best in life and One chooses this reality to benefit One and all sentient Beings on Earth – now and in the future.

One need not shy away from One's love, light and oneness. One realises that One is a 'Bright', an awakened Being of the universe. One is here to shine a light in the darkness so that others will rise to the challenge and find the light of One's own spiritual path to freedom.

Choice cannot be left to chance in this world. One must take responsibility for One's choices and spiritual life. No super Being or supreme powerful divine entity is coming to save One on Earth. If this great Being existed, it would have already come to this planet many eons ago. One needs to stand up, step out and stay committed to One's inner way of mindful realisation and spiritual awakening.

A belief in love alone will not save One, nor will it co-create a better version of oneself or manifest a new aligned destiny. To achieve or co-create anything in this world requires the cooperation of other sentient Beings on Earth. However, One does have the ability to affirm love within oneself through a belief in love. When One believes in love, One is practicing the virtue of openness, which naturally leads to an alignment of spiritual oneness within One's Being. Oneness is the spiritual state of consciousness that aligns One's Being with all things in the universe.

'Being love' is an act of divine free will. Love, openness and oneness are the foundation for all great relationships. It is the basis for initiating and maintaining positive, mutually beneficial and supportive relationships. When One is 'in love' with an idea, someone or something, One feels a rush or increased sense of feeling good within One's mind–body. This is partly due to a natural biochemical called oxytocin and partly the manifested reality One is experiencing in this moment.

Oxytocin, or the 'love hormone', is generated in One's body as a result of certain and specific thoughts, habits and behaviours. These include socialising, physical touch, petting animals and helping others. Oxytocin makes One's mind–body feel love and trust. It is produced in the hypothalamus and released into the bloodstream by the pituitary gland. Oxytocin controls several processes in the body and also helps nerve cells in the brain send messages to each other. Understanding oxytocin will help oneself to take better care of One's health, wellbeing and lead One towards a better understanding of how One's body functions.

'The way' that One chooses to live One's life is as important, if not more important, than what is in One's life at the time of living it. One is drawn to the words of Tecumseh, who lived from 1768 to 1813 on Shawnee Country in the United States. Tecumseh was a great Shawnee Chief and warrior who promoted resistance to the expansion of the United States onto Native American lands. A persuasive orator, Tecumseh travelled widely, forming a Native American confederacy and promoting inter-tribal unity.

Tecumseh says:

> So live your life that the fear of death can never enter your heart. Trouble no one about their religion; respect others in their view, and demand that they respect yours. Love your life, perfect your life, beautify all things in your life. Seek to make your life long and its purpose in the service of your people. Prepare a noble death song for the day when you go over the great divide. Always give a word or a sign of salute when meeting or passing a friend, even a stranger, when in a lonely place. Show respect to all people and grovel to none. When you arise in the morning give thanks for the food and for the joy of living. If you see no reason for giving thanks, the fault lies only in yourself. Abuse no one and no thing, for abuse turns the wise ones to fools and robs the spirit of its vision. When it comes your time to die, be not like those whose hearts are filled with the fear of death, so that when their time comes they weep and pray for a little more time to live their lives over again in a different way. Sing your death song and die like a hero going home.

These profound words are a guide to life and how to live well. When One lives life in this way One has no lingering regrets or doubts. One is able to die well, like a hero returning home to Source. It is important to live One's life so that only love enters One's heart. Fear is the destroyer of One's true destiny. Let fear pass through One so that nothing is left after its passing. Then One will be free, One will be pure and One will be able to continue One's journey in life.

In understanding how to live in alignment, One needs to consider this important question, which applies both to being single and to being in a relationship with another person, living on Country and in the universe: 'Who does One serve?'

Does One choose to serve oneself, another person, family, kin or community? Does One choose to serve the relationship that One is co-creating and manifesting on a daily basis? Does One choose to serve Country (land, sea and sky) where One works, lives and is being present at this moment in time? Does One choose to serve One's ancestral spirits and spiritual Beings? Does One choose to serve the universe?

How One answers these questions will also determine One's way in life. In addition to these questions, Einstein suggests that One must ask, 'Does One think that the universe is a friendly place?' The answer to this question will influence how One experiences life. If One believes that the universe is a hard or harsh and unforgiving place – then so it will be. If One believes that the universe is benign, caring and supportive – then so it will be. However One sees the universe, One will be right. The universe will only give what One chooses to ask of it. It is, in essence, a reflection of One's conscious decisions about One's virtual reality in time and space.

Most successful couples, partnerships and relationships follow a similar pattern of dynamic energy exchange as both living entities evolve, transform and change together over time. Each Being is more focused on giving of oneself to the experience than trying to get something out of it for oneself. The whole partnership is greater than the sum of the individual parts within it. All involved recognise this and are willing to compromise to make it work. The best outcome for all is achieved as One serves the other in order to serve the relationship, or as One serves the relationship in order to serve the other.

In addition to this dynamic energy pattern of exchange, research suggests that there are three key components to a long lasting and successful relationship:

1. Good communication
2. Similar interests in life, as well as compatible virtues and values
3. Shared common goals or purpose, plus the ability to be flexible and adaptable in achieving this life goal.

When One serves One's ego in any relationship, One will manifest experiences that are about fear, control, separation, judgement, hate, resistance to change and attachment. One will know if One is in a relationship or partnership with a person who has an egoic mind because they will:

- not accept and even refuse advice, help, constructive feedback or support
- believe that One is better than everyone else
- be inflexible, rigid in One's thinking and unadaptable to changing situations
- have a closed mind to new and innovative ideas or positive suggestions
- always focus on winning at all costs and think that One cannot lose
- think that One needs constant attention and praise – 'look at me' syndrome
- never admit One's mistakes or feel the need to apologise for how One treats others
- use violence both passively and aggressively as a tool to control others
- always be selfish in One's attitude and actions
- be unable to handle criticism or being critiqued
- become jealous and compare oneself to others
- never be satisfied or content with what One has in life
- always feel the need to judge, comment on and correct others
- constantly look for the next best thing, material object or pleasure fix
- be more concerned with what others think about oneself

- be mind-centred and act mindlessly throughout One's life
- be focused more on the external world than on One's own inner spirit and spiritual essence.

When One aligns with One's spirit in any relationship, One will manifest experiences that are about love, togetherness, openness, sharing, caring, kindness, gentleness, patience, acceptance, non-judgement, flow, non-attachment, flexibility, adaptability, harmony, peace, joy, oneness and balance.

Being a spiritual person does not mean that One belongs to a particular religion or is a better person, nor does it mean that One is entitled to love, joy, inner peace, freedom from personal suffering and the support of the universe. It simply means that One is in sync and harmony with One's own spirit and 'the way' of the universe in everything One thinks, says and does in life.

The seven key qualities, attributes and characteristics of being a spiritual person are described below.

1. Spiritually aware and/or awake

A spiritual person is aware of One's inner spirit as well as One's mind and body. One realises that One originates from Source or Source Consciousness and is host to One's human form (mind–body) on Earth. One believes that One is immortal, eternal and infinite. One is aware of One's intuitive intelligence and how to align with all seven states of consciousness within One's Being. One sees everyone as possessing or imbued with the same divine attributes or qualities as all sentient Beings in the universe. One has an indomitable spirit and unlimited potential in this world. Wherever One is in the universe, One is home.

2. Lives with gratitude and in the present moment – now

A spiritual person focuses on working, living and being here and now. One is not concerned about the past or worried for the future. One lives with gratitude in One's heart and mind for everything, everyone and every experience in One's life, even the unpleasant things that have happened. Being a spiritual person is about making a vision for the future and allowing One's spirit and universe to guide One along 'the way' in the present. One is appreciative and thankful for all people, places and planet Earth.

3. Accepts, then acts virtuously without expectation or fear

A spiritual person is not fearful about life, living or death. One does not allow fear or doubt to enter One's heart. One accepts where One is now, knowing that all things change in life. A spiritual person aims to live One's life to its fullest potential without expecting to be rewarded or the need for great praise. One simply gets on with whatever needs to be done. One applies any and all seven key virtues to every aspect of One's life. Living life well is about learning to live free and being in harmony with the natural rhythm of Country and the universe.

4. Practices humility, grace, generosity and gentleness

A spiritual person is only concerned with being humble, generous, lifting people up and affirming positive gentle energy. One is concerned with co-creating the best version of oneself, so as to be an inspiration and example for others to find One's own spiritual path of enlightenment. One is not critical or judgemental of others, as One prefers to focus on One's presence and alignment of mind–body–spirit. One accepts others as they appear to be and not how One wants them to be. One is detached from the ways of the world and yet spiritually engaged at the same time. One has mastered the art of graceful influence in difficult situations by being One's true and authentic spiritual self.

5. Practices mindfulness and meditates

A spiritual person creates space in One's life for meditation and being mindful every day. Morning meditation offers One an opportunity to clear, calm and quieten the thoughts within

One's mind in preparation for the day ahead. It is a great tool for aligning to the divine Source or oneness. It also assists in responding to the many challenges of everyday contemporary life when they arise. Being mindful means being present in the moment and not being distracted by the past or the future.

6. Open to everything and attached to nothing

A spiritual person makes a conscious effort to work on oneself, improving One's overall wellness and wellbeing. One understands the value of being open and taking time out for inner reflection, change and growth. A spiritual person has an open mind and open heart. One is welcoming to try new things which may lead to new experiences and new opportunities. One is not frightened to fail or make a mistake, as it is all part of the learning process. Being uncomfortable with the unknown is a comfortable space to be valued not feared. Life is best lived not being attached to any thought, thing or theory.

7. Practices non-judgement, non-resistance and non-conflict (i.e. peace)

A spiritual person is not devoid of emotions, pain or aspects of personal suffering. One has simply trained One's mind to not judge, not resist and not react to conflict. One prefers to be aligned with One's inner spiritual peace than be drawn into the drama and conflict of others. One values One's peace and radiates unconditional positivity rather than sinking to a low level of conscious existence in the world. One will act to protect or defend oneself or others in danger, but One will not willingly put oneself in a position to harm or be violent to others. One realises that One is here to act in a way that benefits One and all sentient Beings on Earth.

Ultimately, being a spiritual person means One has decided to live One's life in a loving, compassionate, kind, gentle, peaceful and authentic way. One values being a divine sentient Being of the universe above all else in this world. One has a passion and thirst for co-creating the best version of oneself at this time and in this moment on Earth. One realises that One may never come this way again, so One needs to embrace this wonderful, amazing and fantastic opportunity that is before One right now. One is clearly committed to One's inner quest of realised enlightenment and spiritual awakening.

Whatever it takes, One chooses to live this life as a spiritual person now.

Manifesting a new way and life

Even if One perceives oneself as being in the 'wrong place' with the 'wrong people' doing the 'wrong things', be aware that One can change it so that One is on the 'right way' to where One needs to be now. If One needs to make a thousand micro course corrections to One's life – so be it. Do not punish oneself for One's mistakes, simply use it as a learning opportunity. It is better to learn a lesson once than beat oneself up for the rest of One's life for having made the error in the first place. Life is full of learning – get used to it.

Eckhart Tolle says:

> Stop looking outside of oneself for scraps of pleasure or fulfillment, for validation, security or love, you have a treasure within that is infinitely greater than anything the world can offer.

One has the power to attract improved living experiences or a better future by simply believing that One can and will manifest this new reality with the support and cooperation of other sentient Beings and the universe. Choose not to want – choose to attract. Choose not to sell – choose to share. Choose not to take – choose to give. Choose to co-create a better version of oneself and a better vision of reality to experience now. Believe that anything is possible – so it will be. Choose a life where things just naturally fall into place as it is meant to be. It all begins by recognising and expressing the divine sovereignty within One.

Mooji says:

> Don't belong to anything. Don't belong to anyone. Just be. Feel your Being first and foremost, and don't compare or compete. Just Be your Being.

When One realises that the old version of oneself has been on autopilot, One will become aware of One's old patterns of manifesting experiences in One's life. This will naturally lead One to choose a different path. One will realise that One can choose to be a better person by co-creating a newer version of oneself. This is how One changes the things in One's life – by first changing the things within oneself. One does not aim to change the external world to get the experience within. One realigns, reconfigures and reshapes One's internal landscape to align and attract a new manifested reality.

The easiest way to bring something into One's life is through belief, thought and attraction. Manifestation allows One's imaginary life desires or living destiny to be turned into reality or real experiences. If One thinks it, feels it or believes it with conscious intent and unconditional positivity, it will come into existence. Self-manifestation is also just another way of understanding the Law of Attraction. The act of manifestation is in many ways a spiritual practice if done from an aligned spirit-centred perspective and not from an egoic point of view.

Different people have different ideas, suggestions and perspectives on manifesting. Here are six principles of manifestation that summarise the process. Using this as a guide will assist One to manifest new experiences, new realities and a new way to live life on Earth.

1. **Believe**
    - Choose to believe
    - Believe in oneself, One's spirit and One's way in the universe
    - Believe One is worthy and deserving
    - Let go of all fears and doubts
    - Trust the process

2. **Focus**
    - Choose to focus
    - Begin with the outcome in mind
    - Clearly set One's intentions
    - Ask the universe
    - Imagine the outcome as a living reality
    - Create a plan to realise it

3. **Act**
    - Choose to act
    - Ask the universe for guidance, assistance and help
    - Accept then act intuitively, virtuously and in sync with the universe
    - Live life in the present moment
    - Listen and be guided by One's spirit
    - Be patient

4. **Express**
    - Choose to express oneself
    - Be unconditionally positive
    - Be mindfully and spiritually authentic
    - Radiate an optimistic mindset for living one's life
    - Express openness to embrace change and the unknown

5. Attract
- Choose to attract
- Vibrationally align with One's vision
- Choose to see One's manifestation as a reality – now
- Give what One seeks in the world

6. Receive
- Choose to receive
- Accept with humility, grace, gentleness and gratefulness whatever the universe gives One
- Be open, flexible and adaptable
- Flow effortlessly with life

Manifestation process or cycle of aligned destiny

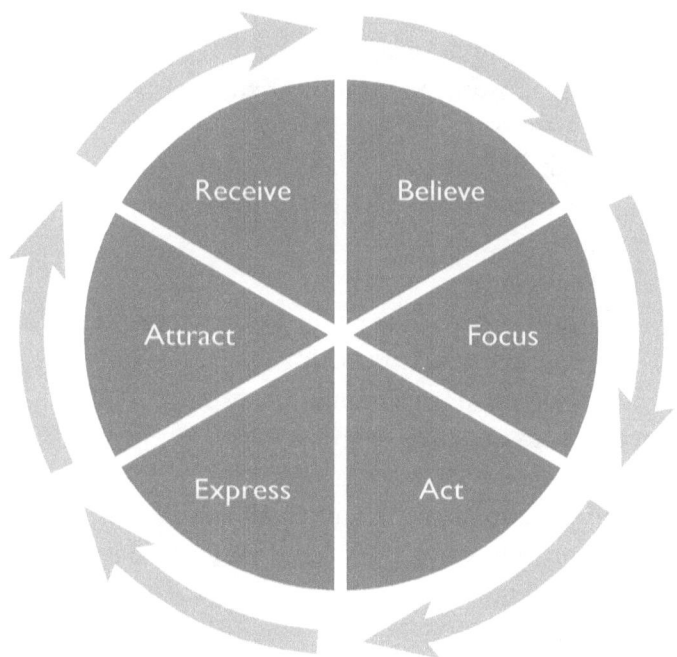

Choosing to create space is the first step to manifesting something new in One's life. The second step is using the diagram above as a guide to start manifesting now. There are no special tricks to this manifestation process. When One chooses to believe, chooses to focus, chooses to act, chooses to express, chooses to attract and chooses to receive, One is choosing to change One's life in a different direction and experience a new reality or aligned destiny. Remember that the manifestation is simply an ongoing reconfiguring and realigning process of One's beliefs, thoughts and vibrational energy of harmonic attraction in synchronicity with the universe.

Let's now consider a manifesting affirmation of freedom, prosperity and abundance to shift One's vibration to a higher level of consciousness in the world. Write it down, think it, say it and believe it with all of One's entire Being each morning and night.

> One is free, prosperous and abundant.
> One's infinite existence is unbounded, endless and unlimited.
> One is enough, One is worthy and One is whole.
> One believes that One lives in a free, prosperous and abundant universe.
> There is always enough for all.
> One's task is to align with the ever-flowing currency of freedom, prosperity and abundance.
> With thoughts of freedom, prosperity and abundance, One radiates to the universe the frequency of that which One desires and attracts now.
> With each feeling of freedom, prosperity and abundance, One aligns and attracts all One could ever require or need now.
> Life's possibilities expand exponentially in all directions in response to every request One expresses

from a place of 'already free, already prosperous, already abundant, already enough, already worthy, already whole, already grateful, already in love, already well, already positive and already believe' – so be it now.

Living life as One's higher spiritual self

The only person who will live a life as One's higher spiritual self is the divine Being who is reading this sentence now. One's way is before One. It has always been there even if One did not recognise it. Simply believe in One's higher spiritual self so much that One naturally attracts this reality into One's experience. It all begins within One now.

If One is breathing right now, then there is no doubt that One is meant to be on Earth. Remove all doubt and fear from One's mind. It is time to completely destroy the idea that One has to reach a specific goal or work oneself to the point of exhaustion to be a person worthy of living a life in alignment with One's higher self or spiritual consciousness. Embrace this moment and create space to realise that One needs to walk away from all of the projected false ideas and thoughts of an egoic economy. One will only survive the insanity of living in an egoic world by rising above it or transcending One's issues or concerns from within oneself. Know that One has the ability to increase One's own vibrations as a human being as well as exist at a higher level of consciousness.

Albert Einstein says:

> We can't solve problems by using the same kind of thinking we used when we created them.

Therefore, if One is to rise above the insane egoic thoughts and thinking in this world, One must consciously transcend it. One must move past the egoic thoughts of economic rationalism that 'greed is good' and the power of capitalism will take care of vulnerable people using the 'trickle-down effect'. One needs to realise that greed feeds on greed and power only grows the need for more power.

Eventually, One will come to the inevitable conclusion that all life flows, nothing ever lasts. When One realises this, One will understand that not even One's enemies, friends, grandparents, parents, children, personal wealth, place of residence or life on Earth itself are permanent. One is continually embracing the present moment now and forever. Life is not an equation to be solved or a riddle to be explained. It is a perceived reality to be co-created and experienced through One's higher spiritual self.

In a world that may appear to be in egoic chaos and filled with patterns of injustice, dwell not on what it seems to be but focus on creating One's own resonance and inner good vibes of peace, prosperity, abundance and spiritual certainty. This is not about being selfish, it is about doing what One can with One's own life force or 'chi'. Chi, or 'qi', is the life force energy or vital life of a living being in traditional Chinese philosophy, religion and medicine.

Learn to listen to One's own inner voice or spirit and the calling of 'the way' in the universe. Too many people are more concerned with listening to the opinions of others and the 'white noise' in One's community, society, First Nation or world than listening to oneself. Sometimes the answers that One seeks come to One in ways that only One will understand in life. Do not try to explain it to others or decode it with some rational logic. Simply accept it for what it is – a message from One's higher spiritual self or a sign from the universe. It is not uncommon for others to respond to One as if One is being a little weird, especially if One says that One has a 'gut feeling' or an 'intuitive intelligence' about something. It is also reasonable if One is not able to even explain it to oneself and simply senses something 'odd', 'unusual' or 'strange' about a person, place or particular plan of action. This is why it is so important to clear, calm and quieten One's mind and 'tune into' One's spirit in this moment. Even if things do not make sense at the time, later in the day or One's life they may make perfect sense. It just happens like that sometimes – accept it and move on.

Know that One's intuitive intelligence is real, vibrations are real and energy is truthful. One's human form vibrates at an optimal frequency, as does everything else in the universe. When One's mind–body is working effectively and efficiently, it means that each of the cells in One's body is vibrating at the frequency it was designed to. Bruce Tainio, a famous researcher and developer of Tainio Technology, found that a healthy body resonates at a frequency of 62–70 MHz. He also found that when One's mind–body frequency drops to 58 MHz, that is the precursor to the onset of disease within One's mind–body. It is also interesting to note that Tainio found that infections, bacteria, viruses and diseases each have their own low frequency that influences One's energy field within One's human form.

If One's mind–body frequency is lowered due to external environmental, internal physiological or psychological factors, this will naturally correlate with One's own mind–body immune system being compromised. The lowering of One's mind–body harmonic vibration provides an opportunity for bacteria and viruses to attack One's mind–body, making One's human form more susceptible to disease and death. Human emotions such as happiness, sadness, fear, surprise, anger and disgust can also be stored within One's human form. Stored emotions are held within One's internal organs, muscles and tissues as pockets of electromagnetic energy and this can have a negative influence on One's whole-of-life wellness and personal wellbeing.

One's thoughts and emotions change the way that One perceives the world One lives in. They are also the filter and lens that One uses to interpret the actions, thoughts and behaviours of others.

It is interesting to note that One's own heart has its own electromagnetic field, just like Earth. The heart generates the largest electromagnetic field in the body. This electromagnetic energy field is 5000 times greater than the brain's, meaning that One's human heart has a significant influence on the body, right down to the cellular level. Research suggests that One's heart's energy is able to reach out or expand approximately 1 to 3 metres outside of its physical body and can be felt or experienced by another person who is in close proximity.

In addition, One's human body generates mechanical vibrations at very low frequencies, so-called infrasonic waves or infrasound. These low-frequency vibrations are produced by physiological processes – heartbeats, respiratory movements, blood flow in vessels, and other processes. Different organs of the human body produce different resonance frequencies.

Infrasound has unique properties. They have frequencies below 20 Hz, and are inaudible to the human ear. They are not absorbed by the medium of transmission, so they can travel far further than audible sound waves. Infrasound can travel for kilometres in the right conditions.

Despite One's human inability to hear infrasound, One can 'feel it'. This is why, without speaking a word, One is able to 'feel' the presence of another person even before directly experiencing this human being. One may have felt the positive energy of a person in a room without ever speaking to this individual, and be drawn to this person's heart's electromagnetic energy field and infrasound vibrations. If One has ever experienced this, One knows what One is talking about.

In essence, One is responsible for One's own vibe, joy and combined energy field of One's human form. One creates it, One attracts it and One manifests it. One is the designer of One's own reality and aligned destiny. One chooses One's thoughts, One's perceptions and One's reactions in this world of illusion. One already possesses the inner awareness to realise One's path of enlightenment and spiritual awakening. One has the capacity to choose love, oneness and live in alignment with One's higher spiritual self and the universe. One is powerful beyond measure. One co-creates the manifestations that One believes and is aligned to at this moment. When One lives life from One's spiritual centre or heart chakra, One creates a field of positive energy that is in alignment with One's infinite existence in this world and universe – so be it now.

Every smile freely given, every loving word spoken and every act of kindness is a reflection of One's inner light, beauty, truth and authentic spiritual self. Deepak Chopra, an Indian-born American New Age movement author, prominent figure and alternative medicine advocate, says:

> According to Vedanta there are only two symptoms of enlightenment, just two indications that a transformation is taking place within you toward a higher consciousness. The first symptom is that you stop worrying. Things don't bother you anymore. You become light-hearted and full of joy. The second symptom is that you encounter more and more meaningful coincidences in your life, more and more synchronicities. And this accelerates you to the point where you actually experience the miraculous.

Keeping in mind that there are varying degrees of enlightenment as One undertakes this awakening journey, some signs of enlightenment include:

- joyful happiness
- peace, calm and serenity
- love, kindness and compassion
- spiritual coherence with mind and body
- mindful and virtuous actions
- patience and understanding
- humility and gratitude
- wisdom, insight and open-mindedness

- great inner resilience
- fearless leadership and courage
- focus on wellness and wellbeing (mind–body–spirit)
- commitment to an inner spiritual practice or aligning with 'the way' of the universe.

The importance of breathing

Breathe deeply and know that One is on the right path to where One needs to be in life. Breathing is a fantastic natural tool for self-healing. It connects oneself to One's spiritual centrepoint and heart chakra. All great Masters and enlightened sentient Beings use breathing as a way of self-regulating and staying centred in the world. Even better, it is free and can be practiced anywhere or at any time. Breathing oxygenates the blood, improves brain function, lowers blood pressure, reduces heart rate, decreases stress hormones, exercises the lungs, increases physical and mental energy and improves mind–body immunity.

Try this exercise:

- Breathe in for 4 seconds.
- Hold for 4 seconds.
- Exhale for 4 seconds.
- Repeat as necessary as often.

Thich Nhat Hanh says:

> Breath is the bridge which connects life to consciousness, which unites your body to your thoughts. Whenever your mind becomes scattered, use your breath as the means to take hold of your thoughts again.

Every human being on the planet goes through moments of sadness, unhappiness or stress. Use breathing as a way of breaking the mind's thoughts and hold on the situation. Simply focus on One's breath – one single breath at a time, nothing else. Just breathe and be now. Combined with mindful meditation, this is one of the fastest ways to enlightenment or to return to a state of inner peace.

Relationship resilience and co-existence

The first and most important relationship in the universe is with oneself. Understanding this is key to understanding One's relationships with other people on the planet, sentient Beings everywhere and life on Earth. To know oneself truly and deeply is to know the universe itself. Learning to co-create, embrace and let go of relationships throughout One's life is a natural part of being human. It is all part of One's learning, growth, development, maturing and socialisation in the world. The more One is able to strengthen One's individual resilience, the more One will be able to cope with, adjust to and adapt to the changing landscape of different relationships that One will encounter over the course of One's life.

All relationships are impermanent. The only relationship that will remain a true constant in One's life is the relationship One has with One's spirit, soul or cosmic consciousness. This relationship or state of beingness is an expression of One's infinite existence in the universe. Nothing can change it, destroy it or kill it. It is more than an idea or concept. It is the defining point of One's presence in this world, on this planet and in the universe.

When One has a high level of mind–body resilience, one can cope with unexpected changes and challenges in One's relationships or other aspects of One's life. It is not possible to futureproof One's relationships or avoid going through stressful, difficult or adverse situations. Some relationships are meant to fall apart completely so One can begin the healing process and reconfigure oneself (mind and body) and One's life onto a more spiritual path of enlightenment.

Relationships co-created with egoic values, mindsets and intentions are destined to fail – they always will. This is in part due to the harmonic incompatibility or misalignment of both people's egoic beliefs, thoughts and actions. Most egoic relationships typically resonant with vibrations of a selfish or self-serving vision for the future, operate in perpetual conflict mode, lack good communication and are more concerned with short-term survival and superficial satisfaction than creating a shared space for the continuity of peace, love and joyful synchronicity. Egoic relationships tend to be a place where people are more comfortable with experiencing ongoing known suffering rather than being free. People in this kind of relationship will be focused on personal power over another person, have expectations that need to be met, demonstrate emotional manipulation or fearful control and operate under the influence of One's own ego or egoic programming.

Overall, there are three types of relationships.

Relationship Type 1

Person A	Person B
Ego-centric [operating under the influence of One's ego – majority of the time]	Ego-centric [operating under the influence of One's ego – majority of the time]
Relationship Outcome	
Unsustainable, very poor to low chances of success	

In this type of relationship, both people typically engage and operate from within an egoic framework. The relationship is in perpetual conflict, with doubt and mistrust interspersed with lulls of quiet time. Both people seem to be using each other as more of a social convenience or opportunistic coupling than a real commitment of loving togetherness. They stay together out of mutual selfish shared interests. Each person is looking at the relationship for what can One get out of it, with little or no regard to what One can give to it. Both people are continually seeking validation from the other person to meet One's egoic expectations.

This is in part due to a lack of self-worth, mind–body pain and a lack of a spiritual perspective about One's divine identity. When Person A does not meet Person B's expectations, and vice versa, the other person will automatically react as if on auto-pilot because this perceived need has not been met in time or to the level of satisfaction of this person. Neither person is present for the other person in the relationship. Both people are incapable of perceiving One's own frame of reference or egoic operating style. Each person is so overwhelmed and significantly influenced by One's own ego that One is focused on the past or the future and does not live in the present moment as it is happening. No amount of effort or couples counselling will be able to fix or correct this situation if both people continue to be significantly influenced by One's own ego. The most likely outcome for this type of relationship is that it will fail with great drama, irrational conflict and possibly self-inflicted personal trauma.

Relationship Type 2

Person A	Person B
Ego-centric [operating under the influence of One's ego – majority of the time]	Spirit-centric [operating under the influence of One's spirit – majority of the time]

Relationship Outcome
Unsustainable, low to medium chances of success

In this type of relationship, one person is typically engaged and operating under the influence of One's ego and the other person is operating under the influence of One's spirit. The relationship appears to be working in most parts but it has troubled moments of significant incompatibility and ongoing differences. There is an undercurrent of relationship disharmony and vibrational misalignment. It seems that there is a lot of ongoing pain and suffering in the relationship. Person A is continually seeking validation from Person B and wanting Person B to meet Person A's egoic expectations. Again, this is in part due to Person A's lack of self-worth, mind–body pain and lack of a spiritual perspective about One's divine identity.

If Person A refuses to do any inner work, the most likely outcome is that Person A will eventually become so overwhelmed and frustrated with the situation that Person A will blame the disharmony on Person B and either leave the relationship or self-sabotage it to disguise One's own egoic flaws and inadequacies. There may be other factors that will influence the outcome of this relationship but, at its core, Person A will see no need to change, be flexible or adapt. As much as Person B tries to accommodate Person A's egoic beliefs, thoughts and actions, it will not be enough to sustain this type of relationship. Eventually this type of relationship will probably fail or linger on in an on-again, off-again cyclic pattern of disharmony.

Relationship Type 3

Person A	Person B
Spirit-centric [operating under the influence of One's spirit – majority of the time]	Spirit-centric [operating under the influence of One's spirit – majority of the time]

Relationship Outcome
Sustainable, high to excellent chances of success

In this type of relationship, both people are operating under the influence of One's spirit for the majority of the time. The relationship works extremely well but may occasionally have a minor hiccup that is quickly and effortlessly resolved in the best interests of the relationship. If any issues or differences arise, both people solve the issue, concern or worry together with good communication and mutual respect. Both people know that One is part of something greater than oneself.

The relationship is flowing in harmony and vibrational alignment as it operates in synchronicity with the other person and the universe. Both people already value oneself and each other and so do not seek validation. Person A and B are equally committed to building relationship capacity and focused on co-creating peace, love and joyful synchronicity. They have a shared belief that together anything is possible.

Both people are present for one another in the relationship. There is an understanding of the importance of maintaining social capacity and 'loving currency' within the relationship. Space and time are created for promoting collective wellness and individual wellbeing. Each person is aware of bringing One's best to the relationship to co-create something special, wonderful and amazing in One's life.

Relationship outcome and aligned destiny

Whether One is in a Type 1, 2 or 3 relationship, there is no guarantee that it will last forever, because no relationship ever does. At the end of the day, the universe knows who belongs in One's life and who does not. All One has to do is to trust the process and let go. Whoever is meant to be there with One, will be there.

Another important point to remember is that just because One started off participating and experiencing life from within a Type 1 relationship does not mean that One cannot progress to a Type 3 relationship if One can change from being an ego-centric person to a spirit-centric person.

Relationships promote and encourage One to live life from One's higher spiritual self. They are also important tools in the self-realisation and awakening process. Avoiding personal relationships, in general, will not absolve One from feeling or experiencing pain in One's life. Without pain, One does not experience growth, change and transformation and become a better version of oneself.

One can improve One's mind–body capacity to respond to significant relationships and life challenges. Being resilient means coping with tough times in One's life. One can achieve this by:

- applying an inner belief that One will get through this – whatever it is
- practicing personal strengths of being lovingly kind, gentle and compassionate to oneself
- meditating on a regular basis to calm, clear and cleanse One's thoughts
- creating space and time to undertake deep breathing exercises
- engaging with One's support networks or seeking out professional help when required.

Resilience is about a belief in oneself and a learned response to living life. It is a way that One can face difficult situations with confidence, knowing that all things will pass in time.

Learn to move through or process any issues, concerns or worries with grace and gentleness, knowing that One is not alone in this world or universe. The universe is on One's side and higher spiritual self, even if it may not seem that way at the time.

It is important to maintain good mental health. One does this by practicing mindfulness and meditation as a way of letting go and releasing stress. Sustain positive wellbeing by nurturing and nourishing One's body with everyday therapeutic care activities, such as fresh air, fresh food, clean water, exposure to sunlight and gentle exercise. Walk, swim, scoot or ride, socialise with friends or family, take time out for self-care. Do nothing – rest, read a good book, garden, walk along the beach or in a park, simply be on Country (land, sea or sky), pat or care for an animal, make time to just be or quietly sit in stillness.

Thich Nhat Hanh says:

> The most precious gift we can offer others is our presence. When mindfulness embraces those we love, they will bloom like flowers.

All sentient Beings co-exist with each other. Whether it is living on Earth or some other planet in an alternative solar system or even a different galaxy in the Universe, everyone co-exists with all of creation. This is simply part of experiencing One's infinite existence. As spirit, soul or cosmic consciousness, One co-exists with all divine Beings at this moment now.

Everything in and on Country (land, sea and sky) lives for something else. The sun radiates its energy and light for all life to be sustained on Earth. The land holds a place for everything to be held in this world. The rainforests and seas generate oxygen for all living things to breathe. The sky provides protection and shelter from harmful cosmic rays as well as a space for clouds, storms and rain to replenish life everywhere on the planet.

All of nature lives to be of service or to serve something other than itself. This cycle of perpetual giving is how the natural environment gets everything done without ever needing to do anything. It is all part of a continual cosmic principle of 'paying it forward' in this world, solar system, galaxy and universe.

The signs of co-existing in a long lasting, resilient, respectful, trusting, loving, kind, peaceful, inspiring, joyful, spiritually evolving, mutually beneficial and beautiful relationship include:

- focusing on one thing at a time in the moment
- doing things mindfully, slowly and with a successful outcome in mind
- aligning and connecting deeply with oneself, a partner, others and Country
- meditating on a regular basis as part of healthy wellbeing habits and practices
- appreciating stillness in One's own company, quiet time together and just being
- doing things out of love and service without expecting anything in return
- being grateful for all things in One's life
- observing without judgement or criticism
- consuming less and creating more space, peace, love and joy
- letting go of One's egoic fears, negativity and desires
- listening to understand oneself and each other without needing to respond
- being patient, positive and generous
- loving deeply and living simply in alignment with One's spirit and 'the way' of the universe.

To consciously co-exist with others in the world means One is aware of both One's spiritual presence and other divine Beings in the universe. Co-existing with others can have wonderful positive effects and great mutual benefits, like being in a loving relationship with another person or a supportive nurturing and caring family. But sometimes the outcomes can be negative and even disastrous, especially if One is living in or escaping a toxic relationship, abusive family environment or even fleeing war or a violent conflict zone. It is no secret that people influence other people when living in close proximity. The vibrations of disharmony, conflict, harm, doubt, judgement and hate are very distinct from the vibrations of harmony, peace, kindness, trust, compassion and love.

The collective vibrations existing around the planet at this time are a result of inherited memes and thought patterns passed down from parents or parental caregivers to the next generation. Most people on Earth have been programmed to live in fear since early childhood. This fearful vibration permeates most lives on the planet today. Think of the nuclear arms race and the weapons of mass destruction currently on the planet. This is the largest evidence and manifestation of how humans fear other humans. It is also supported by the insane global superpower's nuclear arms strategy of MAD – Mutually Assured Destruction. If a country was to launch all of its nuclear weapons the other side would do the same, resulting in mutual annihilation. This sounds too ridiculous to be true, but it is. The world has amassed approximately 14,825 nuclear weapons. According to a new scientific study, a nuclear attack of 100 bombs could harm the entire planet, including the aggressor nation. This means that there are enough nuclear weapons on Earth today to destroy the planet 148 times over. This is just too incredibly insane even to imagine.

Why is fear used as a strategy by human egoic minds? Because it keeps people obedient, subservient and compliant. Fear, whether it is initiated from within One's egoic thoughts or another person, is used as a weapon to control One's mind. The good news is that a conscious person leans into One's fear and space of discomfort. One recognises the fear as a tool of an egoic mind trying to exert power in the external world. A spiritual person with an open mind, who is mindful about living life, questions the assertion of fear before One. One is not blindly led to some false conclusion but is able to challenge the assumption. When One is waking up or following 'the way' of the universe, One will often find times when One is alone, due to not choosing the false path of fear. As One chooses the path of enlightenment or 'the way' and moves along it, things will naturally become clear to One. One will see that the more One moves in this direction, the more the path will be right in front of One. It's like riding a bike – things only become in balance when One is moving forward along 'the way'.

When this happens, the co-existence of One's spiritual presence with others will become apparent. This is what is meant by the terms 'awakened' and 'non-awakened' spiritual co-existence.

As One realises and affirms One's spiritual vibration, resonance or presence on Earth, One will be able to have a great influence on those around One. It does not matter that other people are still on One's journey. What matters is that One is co-existing with all life on Earth.

Living One's inner way now

Suggestions for putting the learnings, teachings and pointings of this chapter into practice in One's daily life:

- One's human form exists because of thousands of years of love and an uninterrupted lineage of cosmic spiritual connections and human love. One is not here by random chance, One is here by divine choice. It is no accident that One is exactly where One is now, doing what must be done or undone in the world.
- Remember Tecumseh's wise words: 'Love your life, perfect your life, and beautify all things in your life. Seek to make your life long and its purpose in the service of your people.'

- Successful couples, partnerships and relationships follow a similar pattern of dynamic energy exchange, as both living entities evolve, transform and change together over time. Each Being is more focused on giving of oneself to the experience than trying to get something out of it. The whole partnership is greater than the sum of the individual parts within it. Both people recognise this and are willing to compromise to make the relationship work.
- Choosing to create space is the first step to manifesting something new in One's life. The second step is using the Manifestation Process or Cycle of Aligned Destiny diagram as a guide to start manifesting now. When One chooses to believe, chooses to focus, chooses to act, chooses to express, chooses to attract and chooses to receive, One is choosing to turn One's life in a different direction and experience a new reality or aligned destiny.
- Know that all relationships are impermanent. The only relationship that will remain a true constant in One's life is the relationship One has with One's spirit, soul or cosmic consciousness.
- Continually be aware of both One's spiritual presence and other divine Beings in the universe.

CHAPTER 5

Change
Evolving as a Spiritual Being

Space to be a free spirit

Between action and reaction, there is space. In this space, One will find One's infinite existence and free will to choose to change. Within every choice, exists One's freedom to choose a different response, a different path, a different way to work, live, experience life and be in the moment. All things can exist in the universe because of two significant principles.

The first principle of the universe is the existence of space. Space has within it the infinite possibility for all things to manifest into reality. The second principle of the universe is the impermanence of everything within this space. For something to manifest in life, there first must be space for it to manifest. This is why space is so valuable and yet so underestimated in One's life, One's community and One's world. Space is a natural precursor to the existence of people, places and planets in the universe.

One might ask, 'What is space?' Space is an infinite field of pure potentiality, where all phenomena may occur. Space is a paradox: nothing may be something and any something is always nothing. One could also see space as a void of empty nothingness with unending possibilities for something to be manifested now as observed within One's conscious cosmic existence.

One's divine free will gives One the opportunity to choose to be free. This freedom allows One to freely exist in any part of space or the known universe. The first step along the evolutionary path of One's higher spiritual self on Earth is knowing that One has space and free will to choose. To be free, One must choose freedom.

It is not just a matter of finding room and time in One's day or daily routines for space. One must actively create space for self-love, self-care and self-meditative practices. The creation of space in One's life is an act of spiritual free will. To be free of One's personal stressors, addictions and suffering requires One to make a clear mental decision to be free. Free of attachment, free of resistance to change and free of judgement. Most importantly, One must consciously choose to be free of One's ego and its influence on One's life now. This will be the most life-changing and spiritually significant decision One will ever make along the path of enlightenment to awaken to One's higher spiritual self.

Thich Nhat Hanh says:

> The teaching of the Buddha tells you clearly and plainly to make this the most magnificent and wonderful moment of your life. This present moment must become the most wonderful moment in your life. All you need to transform this present moment into a wonderful one is freedom. All you need to do is free yourself from your worries and preoccupations about the past, the future, and so on.

The first step in avoiding the trap of One's ego's mental pull to the past or the future is to know of its existence in the present. Being in a state of spiritual awareness is the key to unlocking this deception and seeing through the illusion of time. Be aware that One cannot live in the past or the future, One can only visit them in the present. One's job is to continually bring One's mindful attention to this present moment and the space that One's human form occupies now.

Do not want and do not desire that which does not exist now. Let go of whatever has happened and is yet to happen in One's life. Simply choose to attract all that One wishes to manifest in One's life through the universal power of awareness, attention and attraction. When One combines these three aspects into One's life with the belief that One is powerful beyond measure, One will begin to experience the true power of One's own divinity and space to be a free spirit in the universe. One will begin to intuitively sense and freely flow with a river of synchronicities within One's life. Without trying, One will be drawn to people, places and possibilities of pure potentiality.

One will change One's perspective of daily life from distinct and separate lists, tasks and duties to a freely flowing interconnected energy of harmonic synchronicities. Everything will naturally flow from one thing to another. At first, this way of living will feel odd and unusual but stay with it. Allow the discomfort to pass over One like a cloud in the sky. An egoic mind loves structure and control in life. Spirit-centred living requires One to align with the natural rhythm of life in the moment.

As One does this, One will also raise One's love and acceptance for oneself because One knows that all is well in the world. One is connected with the wisdom of the universe, which is why One's life moves so very effortlessly. One will begin to experience good energy, living balance and inner peace knowing that One is a Source of spiritual truth, divine love and universal oneness.

One has every reason to be joyfully happy today. One is alive, One is breathing and One is present now. All the universe asks is for One to fully realise One's 'spiritual sovereignty'. Spiritual sovereignty is a call to internal action. An act of self-realisation and awakening to the divine spirit within One. When One is fully aware of One's true nature and infinite existence in the universe, One will come to a defining point in One's life about the conscious state of Being that One is now. One will declare, 'One is Spirit, One is Free now'. One will realise that One spiritually operates above and beyond common law, in a non-dimensional state of unending beingness. One will have emerged from the fog of ego within One's mind and taken total self-responsibility for One's life. This is one of the most empowering things that One can do to exercise One's free will on Earth. The simple act of declaring One's spiritual sovereignty by every individual on the planet can make an incredible difference in the world.

One does not need to protest or partition any court for permission to make this declaration to oneself and the universe. One simply needs to stand by One's own inner knowing of who One is now, while other people crowd around egoic agendas and promise to make the world a better place through greed, power, separation and conflict. Begin by looking inside oneself and see One's own truth, cosmic value and divine resilience as a spiritual warrior of the light. There is no greater way that One can make a significant difference in One's own life and the lives of others than by turning on One's divine light of love, peace and freedom. It is something that exists within all sentient Beings on the planet now.

One does not have a specific human role to play. One is here to give the performance of One's life by simply shining as brightly as One can – today, tomorrow and always.

As a free spirit, One has infinite potential to change One's way, One's life and One's destiny through the use of space and time. To choose to change One must first realise One is free. Free of the past, free of the future and free to be whatever One chooses to be in the present.

What One does today shapes the future of all sentient Beings living on Earth. Never underestimate One's power to influence the world, the galaxy and the universe through the simple awareness and realisation of One's spirit and infinite existence. There has never been a better time in One's life than now to affirm oneself as a free spirit of the universe. Let nothing in One's mind hinder, harm or hamper One's spiritual freedom to be free.

Realising One's inner light love and oneness

Trust One's intuitive sense of knowing when One is on the right path to a better place or life. Know that there are incredible, beautiful and wonderful spirits on Earth right now working to co-create a new world for all future generations. There are many individuals who have realised the divine light within One's Being and aligned to this spiritual essence. These people do not live in fear of accomplishing great things in One's life, because One has already realised the simplicity of living with light, love and oneness in One's heart and mind each and every day. One has taken the time to do the inner work to change and correct One's egoic thoughts so that fear, doubt and negativity do not enter One's mind. One is only focused on the positive, the practical and a principal approach to fulfilling or affirming One's divine purpose in this world. One is a vibrant, magic and dynamic person co-creating space to manifest amazing changes with the cooperation of other sentient Beings on the planet.

To know this type of person is to know the vibrations of One's own inner light, inner love and inner oneness as it positively radiates from One's Being. To imagine a new life, a new way of living and a new way of being on Earth, One must release One's egoic fears and raise One's inner vibration to a higher spiritual level of conscious living or existence in this world. Realise that change begins within oneself first.

One's divine light is not to be feared; it is to be embraced and celebrated like the birth of a newborn baby or a star in a galaxy. It is not One's darkness that scares One the most but One's light. Most people are afraid of shining brightly because of the fear of being rejected, shamed, isolated or discriminated against – this is not in keeping with the cultural norms of the society in which One was raised or accepted into. Social and cultural programming over the course of One's childhood and formative years can take decades to undo, unwind and unlearn. One often finds oneself inheriting misguided beliefs, behaviours and habits from One's parents, family, community and society. These projected ideas and ideals have inadvertently shaped One's thoughts, decisions, mindset, actions, and life in a way that was principally fear-based and not strengths-based or light-based.

Over time it is inevitable that One will begin to question the socio-cultural programming that One has accepted in good faith as real, accurate and truthful. For the most part, this information was well intentioned. But One may have felt that there were some important points of inner truth that were never discussed or mentioned for fear of not having the answers or destabilising the 'accepted version of the truth' or perceived reality at the time.

Acknowledging One's inner light, love and oneness is the first step on the path to realising that One is a child of the universe and not just another person living One's life on the planet. Even though One lives among billions of other humans on Earth, One is a special spiritual Being of divine light. Nobody will ever tell One this, so open One's mind and heart and accept it now. One needs to realise just how important One is to life, the universe and everything. Realise that the light that shines within One now has its origins from the very beginning of the universe and Source Consciousness itself. This is why One is special. What resides within One is part of the divine fabric of the universe. Nothing and no person can ever remove, reduce or replace what is an expression of One's infinite existence in the universe. To realise this is to come to a great understanding and knowing about oneself and One's divine spiritual Being.

One may have been taught and trained One's mind over many years to believe that certain things need to be a certain way. If these things were not this way, then this thing must be 'wrong' and must be corrected to fit into the contemporary socio-cultural narrative of the day. When One is able to free One's mind from the egoic thoughts of how One was raised, One will begin to realise that there is an alternative way of understanding life, the universe and everything. When One embraces One's light, love and oneness, One will not be shackled by One's past programming to think a certain way, speak a certain way, behave or act in a certain way. One will be free to not conform to the socio-cultural norms of where and how One grew up or was raised.

In a modern-day culture, where One is rewarded for knowing what One knows, it is difficult to challenge the status-quo with an inner realisation of One's dimensionless divine Being in this world. Contemporary society and science will always want proof of One's spiritual consciousness. However, One's spirit requires no proof to prove its infinite existence – only to believe in One's divine Being.

The more One turns inwards to One's own divine truth, the more One will realise that all the answers are within One's spiritual presence and oneness. When one practices the virtue of acceptance, One is opening up a spiritual portal to One's own conscious state of oneness within One's spirit.

Acceptance is the key to oneness within oneself and being One with all things in this world and universe. Eckhart Tolle says:

> When you live in complete acceptance of what is, that is the end of drama in your life.

No matter what One has been taught, trained in or studied, One's way in this world will be improved when One aligns to the spiritual state of oneness within One's divine Being.

One will be able to intuitively reach out across galaxies and into new star systems when in alignment with the known universe as a result of this non-dimensional state of existence. One will be able to perceive things before they happen and align harmonically with the synchronicities in One's life. One will realise that One is powerful beyond measure and One has infinite potential to change One's life in any direction that One chooses. One will realise that with One's inner light, love and oneness, anything is possible in life. There will be no challenge too big nor change too great for One to answer the call. The only question that One will need to ask oneself is, 'Does this opportunity align with One's spirit, One's way in the world and One's living destiny?'

Changing oneself changes everything

To change or not to change? This is the question that One must ask oneself if One is to spiritually evolve. Embracing inner change and spiritual evolution is about choosing to become the best version of oneself at the moment. It means that One is making a conscious decision to align One's mind–body form with One's higher spiritual self in a coherent state of synchronicity. Know that the universe will always work in favour of One's higher self and best interests. Sometimes change seems optional and sometimes it seems inevitable. One cannot stop change in the world or the universe as it is bound to happen whether One likes it or not. Children grow up, parents become old, and friends or family drift apart. No matter what happens in One's life – life goes on.

However, there is something very real that One can do in response to living life that will make it much more enjoyable. One can accept it, embrace it and celebrate it in the moments when it is happening. Being present is one way that One can bring stability to One's life and negotiate the change happening all around One. The other thing that One can do is simply flow with the currents of synchronicity in One's divine life as it naturally unfolds.

Know that One has a choice to make about One's living destiny on the planet. One can no longer live in ignorance of One's spirit. It is not possible to remain trapped within the ego matrix of One's mind forever. The truth about One's inner spirit will always reveal itself. It will whisper quietly to One in moments of stillness and silence. It will jolt One's intuitive senses in moments of great trauma or significant challenges in One's life. One need only embrace One's spiritual evolution as a sentient Being of the universe. The beginning points for an ego-centric or spirit-centric life path are similar at their origin, but the living trajectory and life outcome are vastly different. One cannot hide from the divine truth of One's Being and all other Beings on Earth. One has been and will always be spirit. The truth of who One is cannot be hidden for long. It will appear to One as brightly as the full moon at night or the midday sun on a cloudless day.

It is important to realise that change is a constant in the universe. One cannot deny it or avoid it as it is part of the very fabric of life itself. Ever since One arrived on the planet as spirit, One has been part of the process of change as host to One's human form. The arc of human experiences from birth to death is a life cycle of change. Being spirit during this process is like riding a river of light back to Source while everything within and around One changes.

Whether One realises it or not, One is a change agent for One's own life. One can become an advocate for peace, love and harmony on the planet by simply setting the intention within oneself and taking appropriate actions that align to this vibration or future vision. One is under no obligation to One's parents, other people or humanity to be the same person One was five minutes or five years ago.

To simply change, change one simple thing first and then keep moving in this direction to shift, alter or reconfigure One's thoughts, behaviours, habits and actions. Set a big life goal if need be, but always begin small. One little thing at a time. Focus on simple steps, simple solutions and simple outcomes. Eventually, with courage, commitment and consistency, One will arrive at One's aligned destiny in life. Simply begin now and never look back. The past is the past, the future is always in the future and where One needs to operate is exclusively in the present of One's life now.

One has the power to move things in a negative or positive direction depending on who is driving the decisions of change within One's mind. Realise that change is a conscious choice, not merely coincidences or chance. One can either adopt the idea that life just keeps happening to oneself or accept the principle that One is the creator of One's life in every moment of each day that One is alive.

When One realises that One is the creator of One's reality, amazing things begin to instantaneously happen in One's life. One will become more aware of One's spirit and infinite existence in the universe. One will begin to develop a sense of mindfulness about the thoughts One thinks and the way One chooses to live One's life. One is like water – One can go this way or that way depending on how One freely flows throughout the day. One will start to realise just how powerful One's spirit and thoughts are and how, when combined in alignment, they can be a powerhouse of positive change in One's life and the world. This may scare or even frighten some people as One comes to terms with this fusion of One's spiritual consciousness and mind–body (human form) energy. Do not be afraid, One was always meant to operate in this way.

When One is truly in sync with oneself (mind–body–spirit), One will align to all things in the universe.

Ram Dass (also known as Baba Ram Dass), an American spiritual teacher, guru of modern yoga, psychologist and author, says:

> Beings who have understood how it all is, who have realized their identity with the ātman, are stream enterers;

they have tasted the flow of the nectar of liberation. They are a breed apart from other people in the world. They know something others do not know. Every part of their life is coloured by that merging. They touch us not only through what they can share, but also through what they cannot share, what they themselves have become. We can only begin to imagine or intuitively absorb those states from our limited vantage point.

To see oneself as only human is a very limited perspective in the world. One has most likely been taught, learned and reinforced this self-limiting belief over time. One's human form, be it male, female, transgender or even non-gender, is simply a sophisticated bio-translator or sensitive two-way interface with the illusions of reality in One's life.

As spirit, One is not human. One has never been human. One's thoughts within One's mind have simply chosen this identity and then continued to believe it throughout One's life. It is a great cosmic joke. When One realises this, One will laugh uncontrollably at the silliness of the thought. What is even more ridiculous is that there are billions of people on the planet who believe this too. It is absolutely hysterical when One really thinks about it. There are literally billions of people all walking around on Earth who think that One exists as a human being who may or may not have a spiritual experience in One's lifetime. The truth is, all people are spiritual entities who are hosts to One's human form. One's spiritual experience is living life within or from One's spiritual presence – here and now on Earth.

When One changes the perspective within and of oneself, One changes the very nature of the relationship One has with oneself, others, the world and the universe. This is how everything changes in One's life. Most people think that One must get the outside right first before One can begin to make changes on the inside. This is the opposite of what needs to happen. When One gets the inside right, the outside will naturally take care of itself. Sure, One still needs to do the work, but the hard part is knowing where to begin to manifest the life One seeks to experience in this world. Begin within and watch how, with little effort, the outside changes too.

Shifting One's inner perspectives and intentions changes One's mind–body–spirit vibrations in the world. The universe will then reflect this new frequency and energy. It responds in kind to the creation of One's new view of oneself, new identity or residual self-image. It literally harmonises with whatever vibrations One is emitting or resonating out into the world.

Life is change; change is life. This is the paradox of living. Everything that is given by the universe will eventually dissolve into the emptiness of nothingness from which it was manifested. The universe wastes nothing. It is simply an expression of divine consciousness whereby all phenomena can occur within altered consciousness or space-time so it can know itself.

Although it may not feel like it when change is occurring, know that when One intentionally changes oneself, One is changing everything in One's life. This is the beauty of beginning on the inside. The outside will respond in kind to this wonderful new vision and shifted or altered mind–body–spirit energy that is being expressed now.

Dr Wayne Dyer says:

> Change the way you look at things and the things you look at change.

This sounds too good to be true, but it is. Know that the future is not promised to any living person on Earth. One can co-create what One dares to imagine now. Just go for it. Spiritual success is intuitively knowing that One is imbued with the conscious free will to achieve or do anything in life.

Journey of awakened enlightenment

One's spiritual journey in the universe has no beginning point nor has it an ending place. There is no physical dimension at the centre of the universe that One can call home. This is because One is an immortal, eternal and infinite Being. One has no form, identity or name; no race, colour or creed; no sex, gender or preference; no religion, faith or culture; no hate, anger or aggression; no attachment, judgement or resistance – One is a free spirit of the universe. One's spiritual Being is in a state of infinite existence. Wherever One is, One is home.

While One's human form may die on Earth, One's divine spirit will live on in a state of unending beingness. Always journeying, continually aligning and constantly adapting and evolving to however the universe expresses itself.

This may seem like a pointless way to exist in the universe, without any 'real purpose'. But this way of existing brings incredible benefits, such as being able to traverse vast distances across space and time, host different animal or human forms, live different lives at different points of human development on various planets, live on different worlds in different parts of the galaxy, expand One's consciousness and experience life in a variety of amazing ways. When One thinks about it, there are infinite benefits for One.

As One exists within a dimensionless state, One is able to pass through any dimension as if it were never there. This is the great thing about being able to do this in One's conscious state of existence. It is why One can astral travel to other parts of the known universe instantaneously and consciously observe life elsewhere. It is why in the stillness of One's presence, One can feel One's own formless and timeless spiritual reality. Look beyond the veil of One's human form and realise the oneness of One's Being. This is the part of consciousness that is able to transcend issues concerns and worries to align with all things in the universe. This is the ultimate synchronicity of divine love.

There is nowhere to go and nothing to do to find One's awakened enlightenment. 'The way' is within oneself. One must stop fighting to find something outside oneself and accept what already exists within One. Thich Nhat Hanh says:

> There is no need to run, strive, search or struggle. Just be.

The key to understanding this inner journey is to realise that One is already an 'Enlightened Being'. This statement may seem at odds with what One has been taught over the years of primary, secondary and tertiary education. Especially as the education system starts with the premise or assumption that, as a human being, One knows nothing and must be properly informed (or rather, misinformed) about the origins of One's infinite existence. The education system goes to great lengths to reinforce the idea that, as a human, One must be taught, trained and tutored how to think the right way, so One can be informed about the right things, to be the right kind of compliant person in the community and society. There is a lack of emphasis on inspiring people to think for oneself. Many simply follow the herd mentality or status-quo. This is fine if One wants to be like everyone else in the community and live an unawakened ego-centric life. But there will always be a deeper calling within One to be more, to rise to One's full spiritual potential and shine as brightly as the stars.

One has not been encouraged to look within One's spiritual consciousness or tap into the wisdom of the universe within One. This inner reflection and spiritual alignment is seen by many qualified educators and university lecturers as hocus pocus that bears no relevance to the 'real world'. The people with this 'educated mindset' only goes to show One's limited thinking and mind centric view of the world. Albert Einstein says:

> Imagination is more important than knowledge.

He also says:

> Imagination is everything. It is the preview of life's coming attractions.

Einstein had a particular view of education and says:

> Education is not the learning of facts, but training the mind to think.

When One is able to step outside of One's own mental landscape or ego-centric matrix, One will begin to develop an alternative view of the world that One lives in now. One will come to realise that One is more than One's human form or thoughts. One is a sentient Being of the universe with unimaginable gifts, powers and abilities. These spiritual qualities of One's divine consciousness far exceed anything that one will ever be taught at school and go way beyond the narrative of thinking a certain way.

One arrived on Earth as a fully conscious sentient Being. Nothing needed to be added or taken away from One. One was simply accepting and choosing another human form to host on Earth. This is where One's journey began in this world. This is the beginning of One's life and experiences here. This is the journey of awakened enlightenment that One is on now.

This is exciting and inspiring news for anyone reading this information for the first time. To others, it simply confirms what One has always known within One's heart all along. One may ask, so why do so many people feel lost in the world? It is because One is still operating from a conditioned ego-centric mindset within One's mind. One is trying to live a life cloaked in layers of socio-cultural programming about who One is as a human being and how, as a human, One needs to think, speak and act in a world that operates on the ego-centric principles of greed, power and separation.

How does One break this ego-centric cycle of governance? One has to change the human living operating system from ego-centric to spirit-centric. One's journey is not to change the world, but to change oneself from within. The world will naturally change as more and more spiritually like-minded people align with each other and raise the collective conscious vibration of the entire planet. Some may say that this is not possible, but it is already happening. This is 'the way' of spiritual evolution on the planet. The stronger the connections become, the greater the wave of change will ripple around the globe. There is nothing that the naysayers and disbelievers can do about it. It is already on its way to everyone on Earth. In fact, it is here now.

One's mission is to work on oneself to let go of all of One's previous misconceptions as a human being and realise that One is spirit. With this realisation, One will be able to begin the process of inner change, inner alignment and inner transformation. Through self-realisation, self-reconfiguration and reconstruction of One's neural pathways in One's brain, One will begin to experience a deep mind-body coherence and profound sense of 'awakened enlightenment'.

The more One believes in One's inner journey, the more it will be revealed to one along 'the way'. One simply needs to begin now.

Navigating a spiritual path

The demands and necessities of life will often challenge or tempt One to go this way or that way in the world. When One uses mindfulness practices and deep breathing exercises in One's everyday decision-making processes, One can become aware of One's own thoughts, behaviours and habitual patterns of living. As One learns to let go of One's own conditioned thinking and reactive responses to life, One will be able to free up space within One's mind to see the direction in which One's life is heading. Turning off One's mental autopilot is part of the process of realising that One is spirit and One is actually living a spiritual life on Earth. It is important to understand that One has a choice in how One lives life on the planet. One can either shut down to pre-programmed triggers or One can open oneself up to changing the way that One looks at oneself, the world and the universe. The genesis of change begins when One is loving, kind and compassionate towards oneself. This is where One needs to start. Because it is the best place, but also because One can and One deserves it.

There is no hitchhikers' guide or defined steps to rigidly follow along One's spiritual path in the universe. One must make One's own way in the world, just like all the other great Masters, thought leaders, spiritual teachers and sentient Beings who have ever lived on Earth.

'The way' or One's spiritual path is One's true way in life.

Know that when One begins, One is already on 'the way'. Realise that the direction is the destination when One is on One's spiritual path. Everything in front of One will enhance or erode One's path of living a spiritual life on Earth. When the necessities of life become the simplicities of living, this is a sure sign that One's path is aligning with 'the way' of the universe. One does not choose more than One requires. One does not ask for more than One needs at the time. One does not try and future-proof One's life from mistakes, mishaps or missed opportunities. One simply aligns to the synchronicities of life as they magically appear and spontaneously unfold in front of One.

One is guided by One's spirit and the universe in how One navigates One's spiritual life on Earth. One's path is about being present in everything that One thinks, speaks and does. One practices the habits of virtuous living in all aspects of One's life. There is no room in One's life for ego-centric experiences, because One has transcended this way of thinking, living and taking from others on the planet. One focuses on maintaining high vibrational energy in how One lives, the way One dresses and presents oneself, the helpful things that One does, the people that One serves, the way that One gives to others, the responses One makes to challenges, the foods One eats and the people One associates with in life. This does not mean that One has become a monk, priest, nun or religious follower. It is not just about abstaining from certain things. It is choosing to value One's spiritual path in life as the highest priority and seeking out things, people and experiences that will value add to it. It is about defining One's own spiritual path on the planet while at the same time recognising One's infinite existence in the universe.

Every person on the planet must make an informed choice: to be and live life on a spiritual path or not to be. If One honestly looks at the world in its current state, it is not hard to see that the world's global climate issues are a result of the ego-centric thoughts, behaviours and habits of humans all around the world. The living trajectory of the planet and the entities living on it is not looking good, especially with the increase in global warming. The projected likely outcome for humanity is to experience an increase in personal suffering everywhere. But this could all change in a positive direction, if people made an individual choice to change from an ego-centric to spirit-centric living operating system within One's mind. If people became aware that One had a choice to move away from an egoic lifestyle and opt for a spiritual way of living, everything would change on the planet. Everyone would be a step closer to co-creating an interstellar spiritually based Type 1 civilisation on Earth. Just remember – anything is possible if One believes it can be.

An important question that One may be considering now is: How does One navigate a spiritual path if all One has ever been taught, seen or experienced is an egoic lifestyle? The answer is simple. One begins by becoming self-aware and accepting where One is now. Realise that no government, no policy, no legislation, no doctrine of the separation of powers will fix what is basically an ego-centric, socio-cultural programming issue within every human being on Earth. No single community, organisation, institution, corporation, First Nation or Nation-State has the global authority, willingness to change or power to face the truth. People would rather suffer in silence than admit that One is wrong. Most people will naturally shy away from the global crisis than face individual and collective responsibility to maturely respond to these issues, concerns and worries.

An egoic mindset will always seek to hide from the problem. A spirit mindset is about non-judgement and looks to create solutions. It is only when One's mind is free of the problem that One can align with One's spirit and the wisdom of the universe for guidance, assistance and help. This is true both of the little issues as well as the big challenges confronting everyone on the planet now.

One must realise that no celestial super Being or benevolent Great Creator is coming to save One, humanity or the planet. One must choose to save oneself. How One does this is by making a choice to navigate a spiritual path in alignment with 'the way' of the universe.

It is important that One realises that every moment that One encounters or experiences is a fresh moment existing in the now of One's life. Wherever one is starting, let it be the beginning point for the next moment. This is how One can refresh One's living experiences from moment to moment. All moments are created out of the previous moments. Every moment in One's life naturally influences what happens in the next moment – and so on and so forth. Through this ongoing flowing process, One is able to simply navigate One's life from this current moment to the next. Moving forward, One will realise that there is so much potential in every moment that One is alive on Earth. Being present in the moment is how One stays focused so One can navigate One's life and spiritual path. Eventually, One will realise that there is no spiritual path as such. One can only exist in the moment now.

Whenever One is confronted with an important choice about One's life, choose a spiritual path. Ask oneself, 'Is this a "good fit"? Does it align with One's spirit and "the way"?' If One can sense an intuitive 'feel good vibe' within One's mind-body, go for it. If One senses hesitation or uncomfortableness, maybe rethink the decision One is about to make. In addition, ask oneself, 'Is there an alternative or better option One needs to consider now? What if One is patient and waits?' Generally, the rule of thumb is, if it 'feels right' and there are no obvious hidden traps or danger, then continue to journey along this way.

Using One's spiritual wisdom or intuitive intelligence is something that One must practice. It is critical to 'check in' with One's spirit if One is ever at a crossroads in One's life or about to make an important decision. It is not just about using One's mind to analyse the situation, it is also about centring oneself within One's spirit. With practice, One will be able to draw upon both points of reference – mind-centred analysis and spirit-centred intuition.

The principle that will guide One the most is that a spiritual path is about flowing with 'the way' as part of an easy and effortless process of living. A mind-centred approach is about getting to the next point of destination. This is the main distinction between a spirit-centred and mind-centred approach to life.

Where there is no obvious path, One simply needs to be it now. To know the path is to become the path. To become the path is to know the path. This is how One navigates One's spiritual path in life.

Being a 'Bright' on Earth

When asking the question 'How does One become a "Bright" or awakened spiritual Being of divine light?', One must first consider One's beliefs. If One believes that One will become a 'Bright', then it will happen. If One believes that, despite One's best efforts, One will never become a 'Bright', then this too will happen. It is simply a matter of One's aligned destiny in life. It will naturally come to One in the right way, at the right time and along the right path. It is not something that is given to One by a teacher, trainer or tutor of spiritual philosophies or that comes from serving as an apprentice of a spiritual Master or guru. It only comes to One when One is open enough to One's own inner light and realisation of One's divine truth in the universe.

Some people need to see an awakened path of becoming a 'Bright' before One believes in it. Others simply believe and the awakened path of becoming a 'Bright' will naturally and effortlessly appear before One.

Now to the important question: What is a 'Bright'? A 'Bright' is an awake, enlightened Being living on Earth. Being a 'Bright' can take many human forms and live within many cultures. It refers to a person who is operating at the highest level of consciousness that One can be and exist on the planet at this moment in time. A Bright knows no fear, doubt or negativity only light, love and oneness. A Bright has realised the illusion of life and awakened to One's own divine consciousness within One. One is a creator of One's own reality and manifests that which One chooses to benefit oneself and others on Earth. One has no need for egoic thoughts, material objects or selfish pursuits in this world and looks to co-create a better space and place for all of humanity. One looks at life with unconditional positivity, potential and optimism. One sees an amazing, wonderful and incredible future on Earth and in this solar system filled with infinite possibilities. One actively radiates a sense of joyfulness, kindness, love and compassion to One and all sentient Beings in the world. One is an advocate for spiritual unity, peace, balance and harmony with all living things. One is not bound by One's mind–body's thoughts and feelings or ego because One recognises oneself as an immortal, eternal and infinite spirit or Being of the universe. One has travelled vast distances across space and time to be here on Earth. One is on a mission to awaken oneself and shine a light for all to see a new way of working, living, co-existing and being now.

As a Bright, One has journeyed along the path of individual pain and personal suffering to be where One is now. For some, it has been very difficult, challenging and lonely. But it has also been very rewarding, worthwhile and satisfying. One would not have had it any other way. At times, the journey will have tested many people's resolve and resilience to co-create a better version of oneself. Throughout these life experiences, One would have had a deep sense of One's spiritual identity and known that the universe is always on One's side. As part of this process, One will have experienced the loss of friends, family and let go of thousands of thoughts and things that no longer serve One or One's true path in life. One understands that where there is loss, there is gain. One appreciates that letting go is not so much about giving something up, but about being given something new. A new start, a new chance, a new relationship, a new opportunity, a new thing or a new experience. One is continually looking on the bright side of life and being surprised about all the exciting synchronicities in One's life each and every day. The universe is an advocate for personal change, mind–body growth and spiritual evolution. It acts only in One's best interests to encourage One's higher spiritual self.

The path of a 'Bright' is as many and varied as the stars in the night sky. There is no right way or wrong way to become a 'Bright'. There is only 'the way'.

It is about realising that One is so much more than the human form that One is host to. It is a common belief of billions of people on the planet that being human is One's only existence in this world. Unfortunately, this false idea and concept is accepted by most people living in the world now. It is disturbing to think that so many people are continuing to be trapped by the mental matrix of One's own egoic mind to think that One is only human. When, in fact, One is spirit, soul or cosmic consciousness.

To become a 'Bright' means waking up from One's 'sleep or dream state' life on the planet. It is about looking inward towards oneself and One's mental perception of One's preconditioned human identity, personhood or avatar. It is realising that whoever One thinks One is, One is not. When One is able to break free of this continual pattern of dream-like living or ego-matrix reality within One's mind, One will realise just how much of One's life has been dedicated to living on autopilot.

One will then be able to begin the cleansing, clearing and healing process to become a 'Bright'. Do not be dismayed or disappointed in oneself if One has spent decades asleep and is only just now waking up to the reality of who One really is. This is only natural; the majority of family structures, educational institutions and social systems have conditioned One's beliefs, thoughts and behaviours. One has been purposely taught not to believe in One's own spirit, soul or cosmic consciousness. One's parents, caregivers or family have intentionally led One to dismiss One's inner intuition as just nonsense. One's peers have downplayed the idea of One's inner spirit and connection with the universe as not real or tangible. One's educators have deliberately rejected and discarded any and all references to speaking about One's inner intelligence and spiritual knowing practices. One's society has labelled spiritual sovereignty, the non-dimensional states of consciousness and the divine realm of the universe as 'pseudo-science' that is based on no empirical evidence. Daily news feeds do not refer to it and if One tries to talk about it, One is labelled wacky, odd or weird. It is understandable that One may feel a little miffed or greatly annoyed that so many people have tried to silence One's inner spiritual voice.

If One is reading this book now, then know that these individuals and institutions have failed. One is validated in knowing that the path of a 'Bright' is true and real. It is as real as it ever was since the first human was born on Earth.

The importance of becoming a 'Bright' is about being awake and fulfilling One's true potential as a sentient Being of the universe. The significance of realising this within oneself is that it is the way to co-creating a new interstellar spiritually united Type 1 civilisation on Earth now.

Lao Tzu says:

> If you want to awaken all of humanity, then awaken all of yourself. If you want to eliminate the suffering in the world, then eliminate all that is dark and negative in yourself. Truly, the greatest gift you have to give is that of your own self-transformation.

When One becomes a 'Bright', One sets in motion universal forces that will bring significant change into One's life, the world and the universe. With this new sense of being in an awakened state of infinite existence, One will be able to shine more brightly than One could ever have imagined. What One does to transform and awaken oneself on Earth is vital to the co-existence of humans now and all future generations on the planet.

Living One's inner way now

Suggestions for putting the learnings, teachings and pointings of this chapter into practice in One's daily life:

- Between action and reaction, there is space. In this space, One will find One's infinite existence and free will to choose to change.
- All the universe asks is for One to fully realise One's spiritual sovereignty. Spiritual sovereignty is a call to internal action. It is an act of self-realisation and awakening to the divine spirit within One.
- What One does today shapes the future of all sentient Beings living on Earth. Never

underestimate One's power to influence the world, the galaxy and the universe through the simple awareness and realisation of One's spirit and infinite existence.
- As spirit, One is not human. One has never been human. One's thoughts within One's mind have simply chosen this identity and then continued to believe it throughout One's life. It is a great cosmic joke. When One realises this, One will laugh uncontrollably at the silliness of the thought.
- Trust One's intuitive sense of inner knowing when One is on the right path to a better place or path in life.
- Acceptance is the key to oneness within oneself and Being One with all things in this world and universe. One will be able to intuitively reach out across galaxies and into new star systems when in alignment with the known universe as a result of One's non-dimensional state of existence.
- When One is truly in sync within oneself (mind–body–spirit coherence), One will align to all things in the universe.
- There is nowhere to go and nothing to do to find One's awakened enlightenment. 'The way' is within oneself.
- 'The way' or One's spiritual path is One's true way in life.
- Every person on the planet must make an informed choice. To be and live life on a spiritual path or not to be.

CHAPTER 6

Reality
Conscious Choice to be Free

Call to spiritual freedom

Choose to believe that all of One's human needs will be met. Choose to believe that One will be guided to the answer to every question. Choose to believe that the solution to every problem will be revealed to One. Choose to believe that One will align to the experience of prosperity and abundance in One's life. Choose to believe that everything will work out for One. Choose to believe that the right people will come into One's life at the right time and for the right reasons. Choose to believe that One will spiritually evolve and awaken in One's lifetime.

One is not bound by any human laws. One is a spiritual citizen of the universe. One is a free spirit with a divine presence of infinite existence – now and always. With these beliefs and vibrational energy, One will attract and manifest anything One consciously chooses into being now. One's life is beautiful, precious and wonderful. One is alive and One's spirit is free.

Know that there is a deep call to action within One's spirit to be free. There is also a great heartfelt feeling to living a life that radiates and expresses freedom. All human beings were born free. All will die free, but most will not live free.

Freedom is aligned to One's own divine free will. However, society has been manipulated by countless egoic minds. Freedom to live, freedom to work–rest–play, freedom to love, freedom to exist and freedom to just be has been distorted in favour of one generation of people trying to enslave the next generation through separation, greed and power.

What First Nations have known all along is that when One enslaves something or someone, One is also a prisoner of that which One seeks dominion, control and power over. It is best summed up by this Cree First Nations American Indian proverb:

> When all the trees have been cut down, when all the animals have been hunted, when all the waters are polluted, when all the air is unsafe to breathe, only then will you discover you cannot eat money.

One cannot be free in this world if One is a slave to that which One is attached. Only when One's mind and life are an expression of non-attachment, non-judgement and non-resistance to change will One be free. Freedom within One is not something that somebody can give oneself. This is because One's spirit is already free.

Most people in the world pay lip service to the idea of freedom, because they prefer to be bound by One's familiar fears and known suffering than accept or move in an unknown direction. The messaging in modern society is confusing and contradicts the basic notion of freedom or being free in life.

It will clearly say or imply through advertising that One must purchase or invest in this new thing because it will bring or provide One with more freedom. At the same time, people are lulled into a false sense of security and an addictive cycle of co-dependency and increasing debt.

This is why businesses introduced the idea of 'planned obsolescence' many decades ago. Corporate executives of manufacturers did not want people purchasing just one single product that would last a lifetime. Returns on investments and bottom lines have been principally driven by profits before people. This has significantly influenced the structure of society in a way that introduces, supports and purposely manipulates people's way of thinking, behaviours and habits so that every person is forced into an ongoing co-dependent debt cycle. This cycle is not about prosperity, abundance or freedom in the world. It is about intergenerational co-dependency and perpetuating debt.

Modern global economies are not built around living a spiritual free life. Within these economies, companies chase increasing profit margins while at the same time transferring debt, avoiding public liability and minimising social responsibility. Even though many leaders will not admit to it or speak openly about this perversion and hijacking of family and social values, it is in fact a form of social, cultural and economic abuse of individuals, families and communities. Another way of looking at it is to see this reconfiguration of social systems as a contemporary form of hierarchical economic slavery under the guise of social utility and living sustainability for families, communities, First Nations and nation-states.

It may come as a shock to everyone, but the purpose of today's modern society is not to empower or enable One to be free. Its governance structures and current socio-cultural-economic-political configuration are not designed to help, assist or support vulnerable people, First Nations or people's prosperity, abundance or to be awake. Society's priorities are to maintain power, assert order and stabilise ongoing economic certainty above all else. Then it looks to manage greed, manipulate power and mask any perceived freedoms in a subtle way through compliant social control.

However, good intentioned and lovingly kind people with compassionate hearts and mindful social responsibilities do exist. These people are challenging the inherited social construct in favour of a new way of working, living and being in the world. While it is early days, many people are committed to social change and willing to embrace an alternative future that will co-create a new reality on Earth.

In the meantime, the primary purpose of the current modern society and governance systems is still to enslave people within the ego-matrix structures and ongoing operations that support human life. This is so that One will train oneself, then teach and transfer debt and disempowerment to the next generation of humans on the planet.

Therefore, it is particularly important that One consciously chooses to be free. Free from One's egoic mindset, free from egoic patterns of living, free from egoic economic debt and free from the ego-centric lifestyle of the modern world. In choosing to be free, One is letting go of attachments, judgements and resistance to change in this life. This does not mean giving away all of One's personal objects or material possessions. However, it does require One to reduce, remove, repurpose, recycle and release things that no longer serve One's spiritual life of freedom. As the complexities of One's life become One's simplicities, One will know that One is on the right path.

To choose to be free, One must first believe that One's spirit is free. Know that One, as much as anybody else on Earth, deserves to live a lifestyle of spiritual freedom.

To be free or not to be free? This is the question that One must ask oneself. The answer is simple. Will One listen to One's inner spiritual voice, which is calling to One to be free now and forevermore? Or will this voice be drowned out by the egoic thoughts in One's mind, which say One is not good enough, brave enough, loving enough or worthy enough to deserve a beautiful lifestyle of spiritual freedom?

Listen not to One's ego. Make space and time to meditate so One can open One's heart chakra and align with One's inner loving-kindness and compassion. Creatively imagine One's future life where One is living free. Know that One is worthy and deserving of such a designer lifestyle of freedom. Recognise within oneself that One is of value and it is important to align with the free will within One's divine consciousness. One is a special, beautiful and amazing spirit. With every choice One makes, One is co-creating a spiritual lifestyle of freedom. As One moves forward in life, One is creating an energy stream of conscious manifestation in the world. Positive attraction, mindful action and high vibrational resonance are all working together to co-create One's new reality and aligned destiny now.

Realise the incredible potential, wonderful value and unique presence One is giving to the world. Look around and within oneself at this moment. Be joyful, grateful and appreciate that One is contributing to life on Earth. Whatever One chooses to do in life, first choose to be free now.

Mind-body pain and suffering

It is not the world or the things and people in it that give One's mind–body pain, it is One's mental attachment to wanting One's life to be a certain way.

Buddha says:

> Attachment leads to suffering.

If One is without desire or wanting, there is nothing in this world that One will fear. This means that nobody or nothing can be used against One. One can simply be One's authentic spiritual self in this world.

Lao Tzu says:

> If you realise that all things change, there is nothing you
> will try to hold on to.

Healing One's mind–body pain is not what it is made out to be in life. Sure, there are medicines and vitamins which One can take to support the repair of One's body. There are also mindfulness courses One can participate in to change One's mental thinking and focus. Healing oneself is about co-creating or reconfiguring One's mind–body to a state before the trauma, before the conditioning and before the socio-cultural programming of family, friends and community. It is about returning to the time of being a free spirit when One was a child.

When One learns to look at One's mind–body pain in a different way, One will be able to break free from the false idols, false promises and false truths in One's life. The modern world tends to project a reality that is very real, but it is no more than a persistent and extremely convincing illusion.

Ever since One was a child, One's mind has been coerced, conditioned and convinced that the world is 'real'. All five sensory inputs of One's mind–body have given One incredible feedback and immediate validation that everything one touched, tasted, felt, saw, heard and smelt was real. Even One's emotions (thoughts and feelings) since One was born were a sign for attention and justification. It comes as no surprise that all that One has ever experienced through One's mind–body senses is within the cosmic matrix or reality of alter-consciousness. This means that these experiences, which One thought of as the part of the tangible scaffolding of One's life, have all been virtual manifestations in the world.

When confronted with the simple truth of the matter, the egoic mind will recoil in shock and disbelief. The ego-centric mind has built all of its human identity, personhood and residual self-image on the assumption that 'all is real' in the world. If nothing is real, One's egoic mind has built its existence on a false truth. In essence, the world is not real and only a vibrational manifestation. Therefore, everything that follows from this initial idea or assumption is untrue. One will naturally come to the rational conclusion that One's constructed identity is not real either. One's egoic human identity cannot be sustained over time and will naturally collapse or dissolve into nothingness.

This leads to a single point of truth in the world – a truth that will change the very nature of One's perceived reality on Earth forever: all constructed human identities are false truths.

This statement will be very threatening to most people. It will challenge the very foundation of One's perceived humanness and the core of One's individual identity on the planet. It may even provoke great fear and significant discomfort within One's mind–body. Pause for a moment. Do not be scared. This is just One's egoic mind reacting to the idea. Stay in this space of discomfort and allow One's mind–body fear to pass through One like the light in the sky.

One may question the purpose of One's life, especially if One has been building a carefully constructed human identity and individual concept of who One thinks One is over decades. It may seem like it was all for nothing. To some extent, this is true. However, everything that One has done, achieved or experienced has led One to this point in time. Realise that One has not lost anything, One is right on time and where One needs to be now. Every experience has moulded oneself for One's higher spiritual self in the world. It is no mistake that One has taken this path to arrive at this destination. One's spiritual journey has all been part of the process of self-realisation, self-transformation and self-awakening into a 'Bright'.

It can be very confusing for people growing up and making One's way through the world, especially when the messaging from the society in which One lives says a certain thing, but One's spirit is guiding One in a completely different direction in life. As a human being, there are clear and implied social signals in families and communities pushing and prompting individual action to define oneself, distinguish oneself and determine One's direction in life on a daily basis. Buddha says:

> Pain in life is inevitable but suffering is not. Pain is what the world does to you, suffering is what you do to yourself by the way you think about the 'pain' you receive. Pain is inevitable and suffering is optional.

If nothing is real, One may ask, 'Is pain or suffering real?' This is a very good question to reflect on. The answer is that it is as real as One's mind–body perceives it to be. All pain passes; it is One's attachment to the incident, occurrence or happening that sustains One's suffering in life. This is why when One changes One's way of looking at One's pain in life, One also changes how One experiences the event. The more one focuses on pain, the more One will attract it into One's life and the more One will continue to suffer. However, if One looks at releasing pain as soon as it happens and doesn't hold on to it, the lesser One's suffering will be. One does this by surrendering to the moment and simply allowing things to be as they occur. One does not judge; One only observes. One does not attach; One is merely a witness by being present and allowing all things to flow in life. Everything that comes to One will eventually leave One too – this is life. Accept it and simply move on.

Know that One's human identity is not real. All is an illusion. As disturbing as it might seem, be aware that everything that One's mind–body has ever touched, tasted, seen, heard and smelled is not real. Even One's emotions (thoughts and feelings) are a manifestation of how One perceives the people and world that One lives in. Every experience with One's human form is simply a manifestation in One's mind–body of external vibrational energies in the world.

Everything that is changeable is not real; everything that is unchangeable is real.

At its most basic level, mind–body pain is a message to oneself to 'let go'. Let go of attachments, let go of situations, events and activities, let go of stress in One's life, let go of thoughts and feelings of frustration that things are not the way One wants it to be, let go of toxic people and relationships, let go of struggling to impress others, let go of trying to meet someone's expectation and let go of being sad, hateful, angry, mad, resentful, fearful or jealous.

Mind–body pain is a useful tool, when viewed in the right light and with an open mind. Pain can be a great learning instrument to improve how One thinks, feels, acts, communicates, lives and engages with the world around One. When used in the right way, mind–body pain can inform positive decisions, positive life choices and positive outcomes in One's life. Do not underestimate the use of One's mind–body pain to nudge oneself along the way to a spiritual path of inner enlightenment and self-realisation. Many great Masters and spiritual leaders have used mind–body pain to realise profound and deep knowings about oneself and the universe. Even Buddha used pain and suffering to explore the 'middle way' and assist with One's awakening. There are many ways in which mind–body pain can be used for good in One's life. Mind–body pain is not a 'bad' thing, as such. It is simply a way in which One's mind–body can receive feedback about One's human form and the world in which One lives.

When One is ready to heal oneself, One will begin to see everyone as One's teacher so One can co-create a better version of oneself – especially those people who may trigger a specific reaction within One's mind–body. One's spiritual intuition will begin to 'kick in' and One will start to experience that 'gut feeling' that certain foods are not right for One. One will be drawn to eating more high-vibrational or 'alive' fresh fruits, nuts and vegetables. One will feel a need to distance oneself from toxic, negative and low-energy humans. At the same time, One will be drawn to positive people who emit a high vibrational, loving, kind and compassionate energy.

It is only natural that One will want to seek out One's 'soul tribe' or people with the same harmonic vibrational energies.

One's intuition may also suggest that One seek or change One's job, distance oneself from unhelpful or hurtful people, spend more time in nature, be still and silent so One can listen to One's inner spiritual voice, take a break from things, read a new book or be with that certain person. Whatever the silent whispers are, it is time to listen to One's inner voice now.

Surrendering to spirit in silence

In the midst of all the adversities, difficulties and challenges in One's life, One must remember to stop, pause and turn inwards towards the silent wisdom of One's spirit and the universe. Albert Einstein says:

> I think 99 times and find nothing; I stop thinking, swim in silence and the truth comes to me.

Know that all the answers will come to One, if One simply surrenders to One's spirit and the universe. This may seem counterintuitive, but it works. One's egoic mind will always try and think its way out of the problem, issue, concern or worry, because this is what has worked in the past. What will work in the future and what will work in the present is being in a state of 'no-mind'. This is where all the great artists, thinkers, philosophers, thought leaders and champions of noble and altruistic causes go to find inspiration and guidance.

Whatever content One's mind–body focuses on and consumes in life, the universe will continue to send or reflect more of the same. If One only sees challenging problems, difficult issues and unsolvable complexities, this is what will be presented to One. However, if One sees enabling solutions, new opportunities and sensible simplicities, this will be reflected back to One to experience. Life is not about getting an answer to a question, it is about changing the question to attract a solution.

The modern curse in today's society is overthinking and overdoing things. Most believe and hope that if One gives 110% effort in the direction of One's desires, One is sure to achieve the experience or arrive at the destination. This usually requires One to operate with brute force or single-mindedness to achieve a life goal. But this is not the only way to live or journey through life. It is also not the most effective way. This egoic way of operating in the world is usually characterised by people having little regard for others along 'the way', paying no attention to oneself or the wider community and only acting with the selfish intent of satisfying One's own individual egoic needs, wants and desires.

Problems only create more problems when one is solely focused on the problem. It locks One's egoic mind into a defined neural pathway in the brain to find an answer. The greatest issue with this way of looking at things is that it traps One's thinking into a set of predetermined thought patterns or rationalised outcomes. Therefore, good thinkers or teachers will always suggest One to 'think outside the box' or mind. This is where the most interesting solutions are found to the questions. In Zen, there is a practice that suggests that only when One has 'dropped the question' will the answer come to One.

There are many ways One can create new solutions to issues, concerns or worries in One's life. One of the best is to become aware of oneself, One's spirit and One's infinite existence in the universe.

Inside the dimensionless states of consciousness within One's divine Being exists the awareness state of consciousness. This awareness state is imbued within all sentient Beings in the universe. It is part of One's spiritual make-up or infinite existence. When One accesses this state through the human virtue of helpfulness, One is 'tapping into' One's spirit, soul or cosmic consciousness. When One spiritually aligns in this way, One is aligning with the Source or the wisdom of the universe itself. As part of the process, One leaves all of One's human persona or traits of human identity behind to access the non-dimensional realm of One's unending beingness. This is how One gains access to the galactic and cosmic intelligence of the entire universe.

Amazing as it sounds, it is true. It is how people reach for and come to incredible solutions – simply by surrendering to One's spirit in silence. To some, this may sound very farfetched and way out there. But to those who believe and have personally experienced this phenomenon, it makes complete sense.

If One's spirit is asking or inviting the universe to help, it will naturally, kindly and lovingly respond to One in the language it speaks – silence. This is not a trick of the mind, as it plays no part in the process except for it being still. It is through One's spiritual awareness that One will be guided to the answer that One seeks. This is One's true and authentic self as a spirit in the universe. Mooji says:

> The self cannot leave you. Awareness cannot leave you. Everything else will leave you. But awareness is what you are.

The purpose of life is to awaken and live as a joyful spirit or divine child of the universe. The essence of One's Being as spirit, soul or cosmic consciousness is oneness, joy and freedom. Remember how One was as a child in the world before all the constraints, conditioning and control – One was free and alive. Free like the wind, water and waves. Free like the clouds, air and sky. Free like the plants, trees and Earth. Free like the flowers, fragrances and bees. Free like the rivers, lakes and oceans. Free like the colours of the rainbow, the scent of native blossoms and the rain falling on the ground. Free like the light from the sun, glow from the moon and twinkle from the stars in the night sky. Remember – One's spirit exists within One now.

Even though there is no guarantee about the future, One still exists with love, kindness, compassion and, most importantly, a belief that good people in the world are now raising One's conscious vibrations and waking up to co-create something better for all. One believes that One can make a positive difference. One will bring One's indomitable spirit to bear. One will affirm One's inner strength, self-confidence and cosmic commitment to a new vision for oneself and the planet. A vision that inspires One to change and do what must be done to co-create a new way of living, working and being on Earth. As One uses One's awareness, One will be able to act honestly, speak truthfully and create openly.

When One begins to look at life in a new way, One's life will begin to change too in this way. Know that the future belongs equally to everyone and so too does the Earth. Be aware that One cannot own something that is an illusion in the mind. Ownership is a creation and concept of an egoic mind used to separate, divide and have power over others. One can only belong to space and time in the moment. This is something that First Nations peoples and cultures understand well. One does not get to take anything with One when One leaves this planet other than what One brought here in the first place – One's spirit, soul or cosmic consciousness.

Choose not to think about all the unnecessary pain and suffering in One's life or the world. This can cause One to spiral into a deep depression. Instead, focus on surrendering oneself to a space of spiritual sanctuary within One's spirit, soul or cosmic consciousness. Find a refuge from the ravages of the chaos in the world and the effects of ego upon One's spiritual self and human form or senses.

Do not dwell on all the changes that should, could and would happen in the world if certain things and people shifted One's awareness in life. Simply focus on what One can do now to change One's own inner awareness and let things flow from there. When people begin to embrace One's own spiritual awareness, something amazing, wonderful and incredible begins to happen in the world. Things begin to change spontaneously in the right direction as if it was always meant to be.

People begin to naturally accept oneself as a divine child of the universe. One starts to see oneself as spirit, soul or cosmic consciousness. One comes to realise that One's presence in the world is powerful beyond measure and simply part of One's infinite existence in the universe. One knows implicitly that nothing needs to be added or subtracted from One's cosmic divinity. One just needs to recognise One's spiritual sovereignty and surrender to it in silence.

Remember this: before One thinks, be silent; before One acts, be still; before One speaks, be sensitive.

Sense of inner satisfaction

Just because One prefers to be with someone else, doing something different or living and experiencing an alternate lifestyle does not mean that One needs to be dissatisfied with where One is now. It is okay to choose to prefer to be elsewhere or in another situation. Everyone has had thoughts, 'daydreams' or imagined something different or someone new in One's life. This does not mean that One is a 'bad' or 'evil' person. One may simply be needing or requiring space and time in One's life. One may sense that One needs to reconnect with One's inner spirit, rest One's mind–body or even do nothing.

Taking time out for oneself or One's mind–body is a perfectly natural thing to do. Self-awareness, self-care and self-nurturing are vital to the alignment of One's mind–body–spirit. Creating space and time to take care of oneself and reflect on how One is travelling in One's life is important to One's inner health and positive wellbeing. Take the time to ask oneself, 'How is One doing today? How are One's mind and body? How is One's spirit? How is One's life?'

Give oneself a rating out of 5 for each category:

Category	Rating (1–5)
Mind	
Body	
Spirit	
Life	
Total	

1. One is feeling extremely poorly or very unwell, needing lots of care, loving-kindness, compassion and attention – completely out of alignment with One's mind–body–spirit and the universe
2. One is feeling poorly or unwell, needing some care, loving-kindness, compassion and attention – very out of alignment with One's mind–body–spirit
3. One is feeling okay/normal/average/joyful – One is peaceful, centred and in alignment with One's mind–body–spirit
4. One is feeling very well/good/alive and joyful – radiating positive energy and being very aligned with One's mind–body–spirit
5. One is feeling extremely well/good/very alive and joyful – bursting with lots of positive energy and feeling in complete alignment with One's mind–body–spirit and the universe

How did One go? What was One's total figure? If One's self-assessment is below 12, this means that One will requires some personal attention and need to focus on improving One's positive wellbeing. If One's score was above 12, this is great, keep doing what One is doing and look for ways to further improve. If One's score was 12 – this is fine.

Learning to be at peace with where One is in the moment is a great indicator of spiritual satisfaction. While One may prefer a different situation, One can still be content with where One is now. Being satisfied is not about having that which One prefers. It is accepting where One is and being grateful for this experience in life. Great people make the most of what

One has been given. These people are humble, gracious and grateful for this moment. There is no sense of dissatisfaction or disappointment, because One is accepting of the situation and circumstances in which One finds oneself.

One does not need the finest China bowls or silver cutlery to enjoy a meal that has been prepared with loving-kindness. One need only be fully present at the moment, enjoy every delicious mouthful and be grateful for the experience. When One honours One's spirit, One is honouring all sentient Beings in the universe. Never let a chance go by to be thankful, grateful and appreciative of others or the moment in which One is experiencing now.

When One realises that One is actually in the 'wrong place', with the 'wrong people' or doing the 'wrong thing', One needs to take action to start to change what One perceives as 'wrong'. No satisfaction will come to One if One stays where One is. It is One's responsibility to do the work to change One's life, world and reality. Nothing will become of One if One continues to suffer in the world. No person will thank One for One's shared pain and ongoing suffering.

One must break free from the cycles of inner conflict, disagreement and disharmony within oneself and with others. The only way to do this is to be aware that One's natural way in the world is to live life in a state of inner peace, joy and oneness. One does this through aligning with One's mind–body's cosmic energy and higher spiritual self. One simply needs to consciously choose a mental mindset that is 'in-tune' with One's higher spiritual purpose and divine light of One's Being. When One raises One's mind–body vibrations it invokes a feeling of bliss, harmony and oneness with the entire universe. As a daily practice, One needs to create a habit of choosing love and being loving, choosing kindness and being kind and choosing positivity and being positive. There is no exact formula that will generate a sense of inner satisfaction in One's life. One must discover this for oneself.

One day it will be time for One to leave this planet and return to Source, just like all the great sages, Masters and wisdom keepers that have gone before One. One will need to leave everything behind, including One's mind–body. The satisfaction of knowing that One has done good things to benefit others is something that One is able to reflect upon before One goes. Therefore, it is important to use One's life on Earth to benefit all sentient Beings.

One does not need to make grand gestures, deliver bold statements or take courageous actions. Satisfaction is often found in doing the small things in One's life with great love, genuine kindness and heartfelt compassion. When One is committed to co-creating a wonderful, amazing, loving, special, prosperous, positive, abundant, awakened and beautiful life on the planet, One usually begins with this exact intention in mind. The satisfaction in living and not arriving at a particular destination is an art in itself. It is learning how to love One's life, beautify One's life and perfect all things in One's life. This is where One will find a sense of inner satisfaction, living contentment and eternal peace.

Everything is within One to realise and know One's way in life. As a non-dimensional Being, One is capable of moving through all dimensions in the universe. One can be present within any space and at any time that is current now. This may seem like an incredible and unbelievable idea or concept, but this is the reality of One's infinite existence in the universe. Many people may shy away with fear from the notion of this pure potentiality of One's spiritual sovereignty. But others will lean into this spiritual reality with excitement and wonder. The satisfaction is knowing that One is a multi-dimensional traveller and within One's spirit is a portal to all places and all times in the universe. This is not a science fiction concept or an episode of *Black Mirror*. It is imbued within the spiritual consciousness of all sentient Beings.

Walk the Earth with confidence and courage, knowing that One is the key to co-creating a new working, living and being relationship with all. Take great satisfaction in realising that, however the world appears today, it can be changed for the better. Simply imagine it now. Imagine a new united, interstellar, spiritually based Type 1 civilisation without global conflict, violence or hate. A place and planet that embraces mindful meditation, love, oneness, peace, harmony and balance. Where societies and First Nations grow natural foods, herbs and medicines and trade the products freely around the world. Where collectives and farmer markets use natural eco-harvesting techniques and safe environmental practices. Where One shares the responsibility for living, sharing and eating One's own food, and distributes solar and renewable energy and home-filtered water supplies. Where people are given a basic living wage and can choose how One contributes to society above and beyond this. Where people are driven more by how One gives to society than what One gets from it. Where people work in teams to improve, grow and develop families, communities and society. Where people teach, train and tutor young people to take One's place in this society. A place that values togetherness and cooperation with other like-minded individuals who contribute to the wealth, health, wellness, prosperity and abundance for all.

A lot of people will not believe that this is possible. Many people will openly scoff, be negative and directly criticise One for even suggesting this. This is because most people on the planet have had the experience of being emotionally or physically exploited, purposely mistreated, lied to, taken advantage of and manipulated at some or multiple points in One's life. This is a result of egoic programming of people in positions of power who have imposed One's egoic will, thoughts, behaviours and habits on others as part of the so called 'democratic process' and 'majority rules' principle, and use phrases like 'natural justice' or 'common law legal precedents'. First Nations peoples are aware of this kind of egoic thinking and the 'might is right' values that have destroyed, devastated and decimated First Nations communities and cultures all around the world.

Imagine for a moment that living in a world with its egoic socio-cultural programming was not the fate of humanity.

What if the aligned destiny of all sentient Beings was to live on a planet vastly different from how it is now? Imagine living life in a spirit-centric way that lifts people up, opens an inclusive space for all to be free and shares a sense of freedom for all to be One's authentic spiritual self. This would give everyone a great deal of individual and collective satisfaction.

The beginning of this change is happening now on the planet. In every moment of every day, people are recognising and understand that things do not need to be the way they are. More and more people are realising that One has an indomitable spirit to change oneself, One's mind–body vibrations and how One lives in this world.

With One's inner awareness, One need only sense this change and move to answer the call of One's spirit. It is time to answer the call and be the change that One seeks now.

Signs of being spiritually sane

In a world where most of the governance, social, cultural and economic structures on the planet appear to be functioning as part of a larger integrated ego-centric operating system, it can feel like One is slowly going insane or drowning in a sea of low vibrational unawake people. Staying spiritually centred and mentally sane in an insane world is a challenge for most gifted or spirit-centric people. Being aligned to One's inner spirit and 'the way' of the universe is a daily practice.

It is easy to get lost along 'the way' if One does not know who One is, where One is going or how One will arrive at the destination.

Given the billions of unawake people on the planet, it is easy to fall into the trap of thinking that the current way of life One is experiencing is 'normal' or best practice for living a spiritually based lifestyle. It is not. Many people will try to convince One that it works, or that society is simply going through the motions of living in a modern world today. People will suggest that One simply needs to 'play the game', 'fit in' and 'don't rock the boat'.

If One feels that One is living in an intergenerational system of fear, separation, control, power, oppression and a form of artificial economic slavery, One is most likely correct. These are the symptoms of living in a social system designed by a collective of egoic minds to benefit the rich and powerful. This type of egoic order's main purpose is to perpetuate economic control, greed, fear and power; limit social unity; suppress individual and collective freedoms; disrupt and deny First Nations inherent rights; and stifle spiritually based lifestyles, practices and ways of being in the world.

One needs to ask oneself these important questions so that One can determine the level of sanity in One's life. Does the society where One lives promote a shared sense of responsibility or aspire to a future by means of continual quality improvement where people work together in the interests of freedom, peace, harmony, balance, shared prosperity and abundance for all? Does the community where One lives actively encourage people to align with spirit within oneself and connect to all living things in life? Do the people around One talk about or honour One's spirit as part of One's normal daily routine and habits? Do the people in the community openly serve the greater good in life so that One can benefit all sentient Beings and act in the best interests of future generations on Earth? If One is unable to answer 'yes' to these questions, it is most likely that One is living in a low-vibrational, ego-centric community of people. It may not be politically or socially correct to make a statement such as this, as it challenges the fundamental paradigm of the current society and governance structures. It is factual and accurate to assess One's current place of residence and society as significantly lacking any awareness of spirit, soul or cosmic consciousness and One's infinite existence in the universe.

It is difficult to have a conversation and shared understanding with people who are operating with low vibrational energy and limited intuitive intelligence and who totally accept the illusion of reality before One now. Albert Einstein says:

> Great spirits have always encountered violent opposition from mediocre minds. The mediocre mind is incapable of understanding the man who refuses to bow blindly to conventional prejudices and chooses instead to express his opinions courageously and honestly.

There is a non-dimensional intelligence or spiritual wisdom within One's divine cosmic consciousness or spirit. It is spiritually entangled with every other sentient Being in the universe and can be aligned to the Source. This is the deep well of universal knowing that is forever present within all Beings on Earth. It can be accessed at any time from any place on the planet. One is the portal to this knowing state within One's consciousness. If One has a question, One will always attract an answer through this dimensionless gateway. With a still mind, spirit will be guided in silence to a solution. This is how everyone is able to access the intuitive intelligence within One. It is not about how much One already knows or the information One has access to. It is about going beyond mind, beyond space-time, to access a non-dimensional state of pure divine wisdom in the universe. At first this will seem strange, but give it time. Learn to sit in silence and be comfortable with the stillness of One's mind. When One's mind is still, all the secrets of the universe will be revealed to One.

This is not a trick of the mind or a magical hypnotherapy technique. It is all part of mindful meditation practices and believing that One is an integral part of something greater in this world. One is a divine sentient Being of the universe and able to access it now. It is as simple as closing One's eyes and breathing deeply, calmly and rhythmically.

When One is able to shift One's vibrational energy into a mindful and meditative space or Zen-like zone, One will be able to free One's mind of issues, concerns and worries to be in a 'non-mind' like space. As One reaches out beyond One's mind, One's immediate surroundings, the Earth and into the galaxy, One will find oneself transcending space and time itself, into a non-dimensional state of unending beingness or infinite existence. As One becomes familiar with this 'knowing state', One will begin to realise the insane chaos of the world in which One lives. One will start to recognise the insanity of people's egoic thoughts, behaviours and habits. This is evidenced in egoic minds of people choosing profits over people, personal power, consumer greed, individual selfishness, personal hate, social separation, attachment to material objects, belief in false truths and fearful attitudes, judgement of people, as well as challenging, fighting and resisting change. The signs of insanity in the world become very evident when One is able to open One's mind.

The question that One will most likely have is 'Why?' Why is it so?' The simple answer to the question is because of a pre-programmed, conditioned or inured egoic mind. Know that a person with an egoic mind will find it extremely difficult to become self-aware or be reflective of One's cognitive thought patterns. This is because One's mind will see no error in the way it is thinking and therefore believes that nothing needs to be corrected, changed or adjusted. This is the exact issue or challenge with all egoic minds. An egoic mind will not perceive that it is the issue, concern or worry – there is no evidence that can convince it that something is seriously out of alignment or 'insane' about the foundation of its thoughts, thought patterns or continuity of thinking.

It is only when One breaks the current cycle of egoic thoughts within One's mind that One will be able to open up and introduce a new narrative or conversational dialogue. A person with a rational or spirit-centric mind will never be able to effectively negotiate, persuade or change another person with a non-rational or ego-centric mind. This is because there is no shared common framework for cognitive processes, thoughts, beliefs or behaviours.

A person with an egoic mind seeks to serve oneself, looks for outward recognition, sees life as a competition, seeks to protect oneself at all costs, focuses attention outwards, views the world with a sense of lacking something (glass half empty), thinks One is mortal, is drawn to lust and need for constant pleasure, always searches for information as a basis for wisdom and power, wants to be a winner or get that prize, seeks power to be powerful over others, fears death, attracts pain and suffering into One's life, continually judges others, complains, fights, argues, has a combative and adversarial attitude to changes in One's life, is always looking to be happy or for the next best thing, and constantly looks to the past or the future.

Now consider a person with a spirit-centric mind. This type of person seeks to serve others, looks inwards, sees life as an opportunity to share, seeks to give of oneself, focuses attention inwards, views the world with a sense of positivity and optimism (glass half full), thinks One is immortal and infinite, is drawn to being creative and solutions-focused, aligns with One's inner wisdom and intuitive intelligence, takes action to benefit One and all in this world, acts without expectation, expresses humility and gratefulness, celebrates life and is fearless, attracts peace and love into One's life, is non-judgemental of others, is willing to act in cooperation with other sentient Beings, accepts changes in One's life, is always joyful for no particular reason, enjoys the simplicities of life and living, and constantly stays focused in the present moment.

Does One choose to hold on to an egoic mind and continue to live life in a world programmed, constructed and governed by egoic people? Or does One choose to be free and embrace a spirit-centric mind, without ego, and live a spiritual life and lifestyle as One helps others to change and improve the world for all?

Know that the spiritual evolution of humanity on the planet is already on its way to where One is now. Without realising it, it is already here. So, how does One know that One is living or showing signs of being sane?

There are ten signs to being spiritually sane.

1. A deep knowing within One's Being that One is an indomitable spirit, soul or cosmic consciousness. One realises that One is not human, One is only host to One's human form.
2. Awareness that all reality is an illusion. Nothing is permanent in this world – everything changes.
3. An overflowing sense of inner joy, oneness and peace within oneself.
4. Alignment to One's higher spiritual self along a spiritual path or journey to be an awake Being or 'Bright'. Co-creating the best version of oneself each and every day on Earth.
5. Consciously choosing to be spirit-centred and not egocentric in 'the way' One lives life on Earth. Being virtuous as well as acting without expectation.
6. A belief in One's infinite existence in the universe. Realising that One is powerful beyond measure in this world. A belief that anything is possible.
7. Persistent positive thoughts, feelings and high mind–body vibrational energy as well as an optimistic outlook on life. Fearless in serving to benefit others and all future generations.
8. Open to everything in life and attached to nothing in the world. Freely flowing from moment to moment experiencing the synchronicities in One's life.
9. Content to simply be present in the moment – now.
10. A belief that everything is connected and all is One. An acceptance of all life as it is. A calm and confident knowing that everything will work out in One's favour and the universe is on One's side.

Perhaps the most important step in becoming sane or 'the new normal' – egoless – is admitting that One may be or have been insane or unawake in the first place. One could have just been going through the motions of living life in a dream state or on autopilot for decades without realising it. One's ego can become so ingrained into One's mind–body persona or psyche that it becomes 'normalised nature'.

One of the hardest things One will have to do is review, reassess and realise what sort of mental-spiritual state One is in now. It is difficult to convince One's own mind that One is insane, especially if everyone else believes One is sane and comfortable with living in an egoic world. Know that people with egoic minds will always reinforce and affirm egoic ideas, ideals and ideology, because all an egoic mind sees is a landscape of egoic values, morals, principles, beliefs and vision. It is not able to look very far outside of itself, as this may disable the false truth and fragile scaffolding upon which it has built its constructed identity and imaginary reality.

To be sane in an insane egoic world means that One will need to believe in different beliefs, think different thoughts, act in different ways, speak with a different inner voice, behave differently from others and live a different life to the majority of people with egoic minds around One now. This may cause One to feel somewhat isolated or alone. But have no fear – One is on the right path to where One needs to be. Know that when One is evolving into One's higher spiritual self, the road or path may seem lonely at times. Realise that One is simply letting go of all low vibrational energies that no longer match the frequency of One's aligned destiny in life.

To other people, One may appear odd, unusual or eccentric when living in alignment with One's spirit. But it is far from this. One is actually experiencing life free from One's ego as part of the natural rhythm of the cosmos and flowing synergy of the universe. The absurdity of being sane in an insane world is that everyone else will think One is 'insane' because One has chosen to be free, chosen to live a spirit-centric life and chosen a lifestyle that is in peace, harmony and balance with all natural living things in the world.

A spiritual lifestyle is best characterised not by what One does but by how One does it. First Nations peoples have always known this truth. To live in alignment with One's spirit and the universe is to live without One's ego. This is One's true path along 'the way'.

Responsible for One's reality

One's spirit is all there is and all there is spirit, soul or cosmic consciousness. One's ego will try and keep One in the illusion for as long as possible to ensure that One does not wake up and see the truth for oneself. Everything that ego does is to hide, cover-up and mislead One from the truth of One's spiritual divinity and infinite existence in the universe. Every game it plays and all the tricks it uses are to pretend that the world before One is all there is, when in fact this human perception is a complete lie. It is possible that One has been living in a 'dream world' for most of One's life. Everything that One thought was real is not. Everything that One felt was truthful is part of a carefully designed mind–body deception. Every experience that One believed was real, honest and genuine is just a cosmic game of hide and seek with the universe.

It is most likely true that everything that One has been told since a child was a fabrication or carefully constructed lie to lure One's mind into thinking that reality was real. What a wicked game One has been playing without realising. It may come as an incredible shock that One has been fooled, and on such a monumental scale too. Every generation on the planet has been tricking and trapping the next generation into thinking that One's immediate reality is 'solid', 'tangible' and 'permanent'. It is no more than a virtually manifested vibration of distinct varying energies for One's mind–body–spirit to experience here and now.

The truth is, what One believes as reality is not reality but a smart and constant illusion. To think of it in another way,

One could say that what One perceives as reality in the world is simply altered consciousness manifesting as specific quantum vibrational energy within an infinite field of consciousness as an expression of the universe. Realise that what One sees and experiences before One is as real as One chooses to believe.

Like Alice going down the rabbit hole in Lewis Carroll's Alice's Adventures in Wonderland, the deeper One travels into believing the illusion of reality, the more One will become lost in it and unable to escape.

One may ask, 'What is the purpose of the illusion in the first place?' This is like asking what the purpose of life is. The simple answer is 'as a way the universe can know itself through experiencing oneself as altered consciousness'. This may seem like a paradox of existence, but how else can an omniscient, omnipresent and omnipotent conscious Source come to terms with its own existence? It is only through knowing One's inner Being or spirit that One can realise One's own divine existence in the universe.

The closer One moves to One's inner spirit in life, the more the truth of One's existence will be revealed to One along 'the way'. This is 'the way' and only way that One will be able to escape the illusion One is in now.

Reality is relative: relative to the observer and to what is being observed. Quantum physics tells us that the observer affects the observation. Whatever is being observed is changed or altered by the simple act of being observed. Therefore, reality is relative. It is relative to One's perception of it as well as the act of being perceived. Reality changes as One changes the way that One looks at it and as One looks at it, it changes. It is an endless loop of changing perception and being perceived.

Little by little, a person with 'bad thoughts' or 'negative energy' can change oneself to become whole or pure, like a lake filling with water one single raindrop at a time. This is how One changes the world that One lives in now. Even the most amazing changes in human history have begun from individual thoughts, unique ideas or personal visions.

Know that One has the power to change and, in doing so, One changes how One engages with life itself. The basic act of inner change within oneself changes One's outer way and perception of life. One is so much more than One's human body parts or mind. These are just physical interfaces with which One is able to sense and interpret the world that One lives in. One's mind is the space for One's human operating system which One uses to perceive these inputs. However, One's spiritual consciousness is One's intuitive intelligence, which is capable of navigating One's way in the world. One is an incredible sentient Being. Do not underestimate One's potential to become powerful beyond measure or a 'Bright' in the universe. Everything that One has ever done has led One to this moment of self-realisation and self-awakening. All that One needs to do is open One's inner portal or spiritual gateway to the Source within One's Being.

The more One believes in One's infinite existence, the more One will be able to transcend all the issues, concerns and worries of One's current life.

When One takes full responsibility for oneself, One's spirit, One's life and One's way in the world, One is accepting that One is here by divine choice and not by some random chance of the universe. Know that there are no coincidences, only divine synchronicities in life. It is time to step up and take One's rightful place as an active agent of change and move confidently towards where One needs to be now. Moment by moment and day by day, more and more people around the world are beginning to realise that the old ways of working, living and being are not relevant anymore. It is time to upgrade One's human living operating system within One's mind to perceive a new way to live a prosperous, abundant and awakened life on Earth.

For a long time now, One may have been wondering why the world is the way it is and why nobody has done anything about it. It is not because people do not have the free will to change or the capacity to effect change in oneself or One's own life. It is because most have been blinded by the reality of the illusion and reinforced by One's own ego that this illusion is 'real'.

The first step in breaking free of the illusion is to realise that it does not exist. As difficult as this may sound, One will need to come to terms with this new reality that everything changes and nothing is permanent in life. So how can anything be real if all things are manifested out of nothingness in the first place? Does the illusion feel real? Absolutely, yes, subjectively it does. It feels very real as One lives One's life on Earth. As One enjoys all the things that the illusion gives to oneself, One also needs to appreciate that One can and will only ever exist in this moment now. One's human thoughts and feelings that One thinks and feels within this artificial matrix are all part of the bio-neural feedback loop that is telling oneself that everything is real. It is very difficult to discount this input and One's conditioned programming over decades.

It is no wonder that this idea, concept and ongoing implications were never explored or discussed when One was growing up. It challenges the very fabric of the community and the socio-cultural values in which One was raised. This shift in global perception is akin to the paradigm shift in global thinking when people thought the world was flat and at the centre of the universe. Eventually, people came to understand that the world is round and it is the third planet orbiting the sun in this solar system.

Humanity's collective thinking on the planet has changed over time and it needs to change even more now. It must turn its focus inwards, realise the uniqueness of being a divine spirit and celebrate One's infinite existence in the universe. Many will continue to resist this new reality, just as previous generations resisted changing the 'old paradigms', holding onto fear through rigid and inflexible thinking until people were proven wrong. Know that this paradigm shift is happening and One is part of this global process of change to improve the world and make it a better place for all future generations on Earth.

Some people are at the front of this wave of change and others are still drowning in the imaginary prison of fear within One's own mind. Staying in One's mind–body pain and suffering only serves One's ego and makes it stronger. The path to freedom or unlocking the door of the prison in One's mind is realising that One is the key. One also needs to know that there is no door, because the whole wall is an illusion in which One has been imprisoning oneself.

As One's thinking shifts to a higher level of vibration, so too will One's spirit evolve into a Being of light, love and oneness on the planet. This will have a cascading effect within One's mind, as it will change the neural pathways within One's brain due to neuroplasticity or the brain's ability to rewire itself. This will give rise to the creation of new synapses, and connections being established where they did not exist before. Do not be afraid to let go of One's ignorance and out-of-date ways of thinking. While One's light may indeed scare One more than One's darkness, know that to embrace the unknown is an act of faith in One's own light and an affirming trust in the universe.

It is important to realise that One is not responsible for all the problems in the world. One need only be an advocate for turning all of One's darkness into light and becoming fully awake now. As One evolves, One also changes everything around One. This in turn changes One's reality and One's world. One's aligned destiny is to continually grow, constantly change and always evolve. With One's free will, One is capable of moving beyond the current paradigm of thinking and of realising that when One aligns to One's higher spiritual self, One is on the 'right path', to the 'right place', to become the 'right awakened Bright'.

This is the new reality for all sentient Beings on the planet. It is the aligned destiny for all those who choose to spiritually evolve on Earth and fulfill One's divine purpose in life.

Living One's inner way now

Suggestions for putting the learnings, teachings and pointings of this chapter into practice in One's daily life:

- Choose to believe that all of One's human needs will be met. Choose to believe that One will be guided to the answer to every question. Choose to believe that the solution to every problem will be revealed to One. Choose to believe that One will align to the experience of prosperity and abundance in One's life. Choose to believe that everything will work out for One. Choose to believe that the right people will come into One's life at the right time and for the right reasons. Choose to believe that One will spiritually evolve and awaken in One's lifetime.
- Know that One's human identity is not real. All is an illusion.
- Focus on what One can do now to change One's own inner awareness and let things flow from there.
- Remember this: before One thinks, be silent; before One acts, be still; before One speaks, be sensitive.
- Everything is within One to realise and know One's way in life. As a non-dimensional Being, One is capable of moving through all dimensions in the universe. One can be present within any space and at any time that is current now. This may seem like an incredible and unbelievable idea or concept, but this is the reality of One's infinite existence in the universe.

- With One's inner awareness, One need only sense this change and move to answer the call of One's spirit. It is time to answer the call and be the change that One seeks now.
- Know that the spiritual evolution of humanity on the planet is already on its way to where One is now. Without realising it, it is already here.
- One's spirit is all there is and all there is spirit, soul or cosmic consciousness.
- The more One believes in One's infinite existence, the more One will be able to transcend all the issues, concerns and worries of One's current life.

CHAPTER 7

Inspiration
Action Without Expectation

Being inspired on Earth

Be inspired on One's inner way in the world, on Earth and in the universe.

There is an eternal voice in the universe that exists within all sentient Beings. It speaks directly to One's spirit, soul or cosmic consciousness in moments of stillness, silence and serenity, evoking a great sense of inner peace, joy and contentment in One's life. In the absence of attachment, judgement and resistance, One is free to experience One's divine presence within One's spirit. As spirit, everyone has infinite free will to spiritually align One's living intention with 'the way' of the universe. The first simple step along this inner journey begins where One is now. Simply set One's intention to be all that One can be.

At the centre of each person's journey is a sentient Being. Within this Being is a divine spirit of infinite existence. As spirit, One is host to One's mind and body. Everyone's journey as a spiritual Being is about experiencing One's human form within a field of infinite possibilities. To truly and deeply know One's way in this world is to transition away from the matrix of mindless thinking, doing, speaking, seeking, wanting, reacting, controlling and manipulating. Co-create an intuitive approach that embraces healthy habits, such as meditation, mindful living and a spirit-centred way of just being now.

Inspire oneself with enlightened confidence in One's divine spirit and trust in the universe. When One lets go of One's mind's contemporary fears, consuming anxieties and insatiable thirsts for more and more things in One's life, One will be free to reawaken to One's inner truth and spirit.

Through a commitment to being compassionate, helpful, accepting, generous, simple, patient and open, One is able to co-create the best version of oneself on Earth. The inspiring teachings, learnings and pointings in this book allow One to stop limiting thoughts, beliefs and behaviours, and start experiencing a Source-aligned life that is manifested in the present moment and centred within One's spirit.

Know that when One changes the way that One looks at oneself and One's life, then amazing things begin to change and manifest in One's life too.

Now is the right moment to awaken One's spirit and co-create an enlightened life of spirit-centred mindful living.

As One walks One's own path in life know that One's journey on the planet is not the same as others. There will be moments of shared togetherness but at other times One will need to journey by oneself. But if One has the good fortune to meet along 'the way', acknowledge, encourage and inspire others in this moment. Know that all connections are temporary and will eventually end one day. Find comfort and inspiration in One's own journey, because it too will end in the same way which One came into the world – as spirit, soul or cosmic consciousness. Learn how to 'make a life' for oneself within the fluctuating patterns of energy, place-based plans, personal priorities and chaos of the world.

It is time to inspire oneself to speak One's truth in the world, so One can shine a divine light of inner change to co-create a new Earth – an Earth that is spiritually united into an interstellar Type 1 civilisation to benefit all generations of humans, now and in the future. This act of inner courage and inspiration will likely trigger a lot of people with mediocre minds, but One will free more spiritual Beings than One can possibly imagine. There will be people with change-ready minds who will accept, and other minds still in the process of letting go or escaping One's egoic mental matrix. Know that what One does today matters.

Stay centred within One's spirit, be open and truthful, be honest and genuine, be raw but real, be gentle and sensitive, be bold and courageous, be positive and express One's inner joy, love, light and oneness in this world. Realise that One's vibrations will echo out across the world and into the universe like ripples on a pond. One's life signature and living energy will always attract those who are of a similar energy pattern. This will naturally draw One's kind, tribe, mob – people who hold the same depth, understand and vision of One's spirit to oneself. The right type of people will always find One in the world, and those who are not will fade from One's circle of trust.

One may ask, 'How does One inspire oneself on Earth?' The answer is simple: 'Believe'. Believe in oneself and One's indomitable spirit to change oneself and, in doing so, change the world. Believe that anything is possible and that everything changes in life. Believe that One possesses power beyond measure and the capacity for good in this world. Believe that every day One is alive, One's living signature, 'chi' or life force energy is able to influence all things around oneself and people in different parts of the world. Believe that people of Earth are all part of a spiritual evolutionary process even though

One may not realise it now. Believe that what One does today matters.

All One has to do is to continue to be and express One's unique authentic spiritual self in the world. Trust the universe to take care of itself. In the meantime, One needs to take care of One's mind–body–spirit and life.

One is already imbued with seven states of consciousness within One's spirit. One has the infinite potential to do something amazing and beautiful on this planet and in the universe. One simply needs to tap into this inner cosmic confidence and become motivated to act with spiritual intuition as if by a supernatural force or divine influence.

When One is finally able to break free and dissolve the attachment to One's ego within One's mind, One will realise how it has been holding oneself back for all these years or decades. One might even wonder why someone didn't teach One about this egoic matrix and mental conditioning within One's mind. Most of society, professors, professional educators, teachers, trainers and tutors are still living in an unawake or dream state. These so-called qualified people can only teach what One perceives as One's own reality – even if it is a false truth.

Be patient with these people, as they are still living in the illusion of life. It may not be One's time to wake up, and it cannot be forced upon these individuals. One must journey to this place of self-realisation and awakening for oneself. As much as One would like to inspire others to 'wake up', One can only lead by example and encourage others to do the same. The evidence of the benefits of living an 'awake life' is overwhelming. It reduces stress and taps directly into the Source for all things in the universe. It creates a paradigm shift in One's belief system. This becomes a catalyst for changes in how One sees oneself in the world and the universe. Another effect will be reduced pain and suffering in One's life.

It will also influence One's relationships with others through a shift in One's overall vibrational energy. It can sometimes have a dramatic effect on people, like two magnets of the same polarity pushing one another away with an invisible force. Do not be concerned if this has happened to oneself or is indeed happening. It is all part of the synchronicity and harmonic alignment within the universe. Simply remain open and allow it to happen. Stay present in the moment and continue to have a positive outlook on life as it unfolds naturally and spontaneously.

Know that the universe does not want One to try harder, be more committed or make some kind of grand gesture. It simply invites One to trust it more in moments of doubt and indecision and with One's life. When One is able to realise that the obstacle is the path, One's path will become clear. Know that the universe and truth have no agenda.

Focus not on the absence of things, people or experiences in One's life. Instead consciously choose to focus on these living manifestations being present in One's life now. Inspire oneself with the idea that wonderful things come easily and effortlessly into One's life. Know that One is very capable of co-creating the life One imagines and chooses to manifest as One's reality. Just because One's path to this point in life may have been difficult or challenging, this does not mean that One is not worthy – One is truly worthy. Believe in oneself and the idea that very soon all things that are meant to come to One will manifest in One's life as One's reality. This is inspired thinking; it all begins with an inspired belief to co-create a different reality now on Earth. Know that the way One sees oneself helps shape and influence how One treats oneself, people and the world One lives in.

Take the time to create space in One's life to inspire a sense of freedom. Realise that One is 'no-thing' and requires nothing in this life to be free. Freedom is therefore within One and One need only inspire oneself to transcend all false truths about oneself to see it now. As a sentient Being of the universe, One is already beyond achieving anything or impressing anyone in life. Remember why One is here now – to be present and awake. Within this space and time on Earth, One is able to inspire humanity with One's own light, love and oneness as an interstellar cosmic traveller. When One inspires with love, One transcends all human experiences with a sense of divine intervention. In the pure essence of One's spirit, soul or cosmic consciousness, there is only light and oneness. One is even free of the idea of light and oneness in this state of infinite existence.

Choose to be a guiding light of divine inspiration with One's own life in this world. Know that great spirits do not fear time or the challenge before One. Shine as brightly as One can and exist now.

Living practice and spiritual habits

Life is a practice. What One does each day, One becomes. The more One is able to observe One's mind and life each day, the more One will be able to create a living practice to improve, beautify and perfect all things in One's life. With every step One takes along One's spiritual journey in life, the closer One is aligned with One spirit, soul or cosmic consciousness in the universe. New opportunities do not magically fall from the sky but may sometimes appear in front of One. The best way to ensure One's life path and direction is to go out into the world and make it happen, preferably from an inner place and space of calmness, stillness and peace. When One is able to 'get it right' or 'reconfigure' One's mental landscape on the inside, the outside will naturally take care of itself.

Therefore, begin within oneself to make tiny changes in One's thoughts, how One sees oneself and where One wants to be in the world. Spiritual practice shows One the way back to oneself or One's spirit. It is not meant to be an escape from life, an acquisition of divine essence or possession of hidden secrets. Spiritual practice is an alignment with the harmony and natural synergy of the universe in the way One thinks, speaks and acts towards oneself and others on the planet. Do not be concerned with other's behaviours, instead focus on how One can be present in the moment. One's daily outcome should be to live a life that is true to One's spiritual practice, beliefs and virtues.

One may have found that, in the past, One was attracted to people with traumatic, toxic and negative energy who were replaying a victim mindset and harmful narratives of hurt and helplessness. However, as One heals and changes One's inner language and story from hopelessness to a new narrative of light, love and oneness, One's life will begin to experience an exciting new living reality. Remember that One is only a 'victim' if One chooses to be. Personal pain and ongoing suffering are not a prerequisite for living on Earth. Choose a reality where One is the hero of One's story and the captain of One's divine destiny in life.

More and more people around the world are giving up the old ways of looking at One's life and the world with despair and desperateness. People are being magically drawn to others who are in alignment with One's spirit, soul or cosmic consciousness. It is no coincidence that people are searching and seeking for a new way to live life that transcends the old social doctrines of control, conservativism and containment. Cruelty and unkindness are not cures for the current condition of the world and Earth. The only recipe for changing to a new reality is a spiritual practice that embraces inner kindness, care and compassion.

One will only move to a new future if One willingly chooses to move oneself now. The currents of change are always moving One along the river of life. The trick is not to fight it, but to flow with it and steer One's own course or path. It is time to give up One's old ego-centric lifestyle and embrace a new spirit-centric living wellness in One's community. When One makes this conscious decision to change, One's existing friends or family will naturally view One with suspicion and think that One has gone 'insane' or become a new age eccentric or social oddity. Fear not, this is a completely natural reaction from people who are locked within an egoic framework and perspective. To people who have been brought up living, thinking and acting in alignment with an egoic mindset, this is all One knows how to do. This is One's only point of reference in life and anything that occurs outside this conditioned programming is completely 'alien' or foreign to One's mental and physical landscape. It is incredibly difficult and extremely challenging for a person with an egoic mindset to let go and consider alternative perspectives, especially a spiritual outlook. A person with a spiritual mindset is able to embrace all perspectives. Know that those people who are truly meant to be in One's life will be.

Do not be discouraged if One is finding significant mental resistance to breaking free or letting go of One's egoic mindset. It is undoubtedly the ultimate life challenge of One's existence on Earth. It is One's spiritual journey or vision quest, which must be conquered only by oneself and in the silent presence of One's mind–body–spirit. When One has finally 'killed' or disentangled One's attachment to One's ego – only then will One be free.

Eckhart Tolle says:

> The mind is using you. You are unconsciously identified with it, so you don't even know that you are its slave. It's almost as if you were possessed without knowing it, and so you take the possessing entity to be yourself. The beginning of freedom is the realization that you are not the possessing entity – the thinker. Knowing this enables you to observe the entity. The moment you start watching the thinker, a higher level of consciousness becomes activated. You then begin to realize that there is a vast realm of intelligence beyond thought, that thought is only a tiny aspect of that intelligence.

When One is able to move beyond One's egoic mind, One will realise One's spirit, soul or cosmic consciousness within One. It has been there all along, ever since One was a baby within One's mother's womb when One came to this planet. One arrived as spirit and synergised as a host to One's human form. Realise that One as spirit is actually without gender, race, cultural identity, age, DNA, social status, time, form or anything that One can call human. If fact, One is not human at all and has never been. All the social labels and conditioning are a construct of what has been applied onto and uploaded into One's human residual imaging or personhood within One's mind. The reality that One calls life has all been made up over the course of One's lifetime. One is simply a spiritual entity operating as a human avatar in a world filled with other avatars. The problem arises when One actually believes that One is the avatar and not the spiritual Being or operator being the human avatar. This is when things become complicated in the world.

Eventually One will realise that there are billions of human avatars who are in 'sleep mode' or unawake people all going about One's daily lives thinking that this is all there is. Not realising that One is actually a spiritual Being or cosmic consciousness operating in silence behind One's personal human form or artificial avatar.

As One becomes more and more aware of One as spirit and One's human avatar or mind–body, One will be able to create a spiritual practice that aligns with One's spirit and 'the way' of the universe. One will begin to see how, with little effort, One will be able to put into practice a way of thinking, living and being with life that flows effortlessly and easily throughout the day. One will start to 'consciously and intuitively flow' with life, which is easy, less stressful and more personally rewarding. One's attention will move away from problems, issues, concerns and worries to seeing opportunities, creating solutions and embracing the living joy of life. One will not resist change but see it as something to be moved through as part of a living process. As One becomes more and more present in the moment, One will find that One is able to align with all seven states of consciousness within One's spiritual

Being. One will be able to 'tap into', 'turn on' or align to the distinct states of consciousness within One to guide and support One's spiritual practice in life. Spiritual practice is not a religious dogma that must be followed without question. It is a way of knowing oneself so that there is 'no-self', only the purity of One's spiritual sovereignty or divinity in the world and universe.

Spiritual habits are behaviours that support One's spiritual practice. It is important to have daily habits that keep One grounded, mindful and focused on being present and virtuous. Spiritual virtues such as the seven key virtues – compassion, helpfulness, acceptance, simplicity, patience, generosity and openness – help One open a spiritual gateway to various states of consciousness within One. Mindful meditation plays an important role in focusing the mind and letting go of all things that no longer serve One.

Atisha Dipankara Shrijnana (982–1052 CE), a Buddhist monk credited with reforming Tibetan Buddhism, says:

> The greatest achievement is selflessness.
> The greatest worth is self-mastery.
> The greatest quality is seeking to serve others.
> The greatest precept is continual awareness.
> The greatest medicine is the emptiness of everything.
> The greatest action is not conforming with the world's ways.
> The greatest magic is transmuting the passions.
> The greatest generosity is non-attachment.
> The greatest goodness is a peaceful mind.
> The greatest patience is humility.
> The greatest effort is not concerned with results.
> The greatest meditation is a mind that lets go.
> The greatest wisdom is seeing through appearances.

As One focuses One's life on One's daily spiritual habits, these habits will merge into One's living practice and develop like a blossoming tree bearing fruit all year long. Little by little, as One nurtures and nourishes One's individual habits, this practice will have a profound effect and influence on the people in One's life. It will create a ripple or wave of spiritual consciousness that will radiate out from oneself into the world around One. One will experience an increase in One's positive vibrational energy in proportion to One's alignment with One's higher spiritual self. There will be moments when One will feel extreme inner joy, contentment and peace, regardless of what possessions, material objects, income, wealth or relationships One has in One's life.

As One stays in alignment throughout the day, all the answers will come to One like water flowing from a river to the ocean. All the answers already exist to every question One has in life. One need only immerse oneself in the still waters of Source Consciousness through 'real-time' meditation to access One's intuitive intelligence and the wisdom of the universe. Nothing is hidden when One is completely open, transparent and free.

Time to transmute, transform and transcend

It is not appropriate, fair or reasonable to expect others to love oneself exactly the way that One wants, desires or needs to be loved. Relationships between people are not places to have or to hold unrealistic standards, behaviours or actions for others to meet when One does not place those same attitudes, conditions or outcomes upon oneself. A relationship is a sacred space for shared unity, harmony, balance, love, conscious fusion of presence, mind–body–spirit synergy, mindful living, cosmic togetherness and oneness. It is a place for bringing out the best in others and serving the greater good of the relationship, family, community, First Nation, world and universe.

It is One's responsibility to be the best loving version of oneself, which will naturally attract the love that aligns and harmonises with One's vibrational energy in the world. Choose not to be a superficial version of oneself in life. Have the courage, kindness and commitment to be One's authentic, beautiful and loving spiritual self.

Know that all great love is founded on vibrational attraction and spiritual alignment not superficial beauty or temporary transactions of pleasure. Osho says:

> Those who have found the source of love within themselves are no longer in need of love. And they will be loved. They will love for no other reason but simply because they have too much of it – just as a rain cloud wants to rain, just as a flower wants to release its fragrance, with no desire to get anything. The reward of love is in loving, not in getting love.

The main difference is that a person with an ego-centric mind will always choose to want love and affection whereas a person with a spirit-centred mind will choose to give love and affection first without expecting anything in return, because this is who One chooses to be in life. People can spend a lifetime looking for that 'right person' only to realise that the love One is seeking was within oneself all along. Another person will only ever reflect what One chooses to be in this life. This is how harmonic attraction and the natural synergy of the universe works all around the world. Therefore, 'being love', or being in the conscious state of oneness, is a way of life that is in alignment with all living things on Country (land, sea and sky).

Know that every relationship with another Being is an opportunity and every person is a gift to align with One's higher spiritual self. When One is in alignment, One will experience:

- higher brain function or synaptic connectivity, great memory recall and increased clarity
- advanced imagination and visualisation of a new reality or future

- the ability to communicate or express oneself intelligently and verbally with purposeful intent
- lack of fear and resistance to change, grow and transform oneself
- increased ability to connect to One's intuitive intelligence – mind–body–spirit
- balanced sexual energy within oneself
- heightened feelings of being connected to the world or oneness with all living things.

As One transforms from a place stuck in the past to a new imagined living and vibrant space in the present, One will realise that One has incredible transmuting powers to change One's old perspectives, energies and outlook to something new in the world today. To heal is to change; to change is to transform One's inner relationship with oneself and thus co-create a new reality for living life. Noticeable signs that One is changing in the right way will be when One observes more; judges less, mindfully responds more; reacts less, gives self-love more; self-sabotages less, creates care kindness and compassionate boundaries more; meets expectations less, focuses on inner peace more; experiences outer chaos less, brings greater clarity more; dwells in confusion less, simply being more; does less, believes in faith more; fears less, stands up with courage more; sits down in shame less, demonstrates greatness from within more; dims One's inner light less. These symptoms or signs of change can and will have a great positive effect on One's life and those that One is connected to in the community. Do not underestimate One's individual power to change oneself and indeed the world.

Life is too short to be a prisoner of the past and stuck in repeating patterns of personal pain and suffering. Let go of any and all drama in One's life now. It is okay to step back and create a bubble of conscious awareness and personal protective boundaries for oneself. When One finally makes the decision to not live a fake life with false friends and family, One will need to unconditionally accept all that is now without being drawn into the social vortex of fabrication, the illusion of reality and cosmic chaos. With unconditional acceptance, One will realise the impermanence of everything. All things change over time – no person escapes One's own death. All One can do is prepare for it when it comes and die like a hero going home.

One as a spirit is an observer of One's human form. Over One's entire lifetime on Earth, One will be present in every moment of every day and every year that One is alive. Know that One's human form is either in the:

- co-creating process of life (assembling or constructing of DNA and human form)
- living process of life (engaging or interacting)
- dying process of life (deconstructing).

The universe wastes nothing; all matter and energy is simply transformed. This is the simplicity and divine beauty of existing within an infinite field of pure potentiality – everything is possible, all things are probable.

To transmute, transform and transcend One's current life and lifestyle One must be willing to believe and see a new reality. Not some mystical image surrounded in fairy lights or fuzzy feelings, but an imagined experience as real as the sun's rays on One's skin or the air that One breathes. Begin by getting into the mindset where One willingly attracts something wonderful, unexpected and amazing to happen in One's life. Like a sudden win-win-win shift or an out-of-the-blue miracle of divine synchronicity. Allow for the possibility of an instant breakthrough in whatever One is focusing on in One's life. Remove any preconceived notions of a particular outcome or how One thinks things will unfold or happen. Just let go of the outcome and trust the process of the universe to give what is already on its way to One. In short, trust more, believe more, receive more.

Say to the universe, 'One is open, ready and willing to receive all divine gifts of the universe. One is grateful for everything and everyone in One's life, One gives unconditional gratitude, love and thanks for One's prosperity, abundance and wakefulness ... as One aligns to One's higher spiritual self now.'

As One moves from 'wanting' mode to 'attracting' mode, One creates a temporal shift in space-time along with the conscious relationship One has with the universe. The universe is not something that One 'gets' things from, but an infinite Source from which it 'gives' things, people and experiences to oneself. To activate attraction mode in One's life, One must believe in One's own intuitive intelligence, intentionally aligned reality or purposeful visioning and spiritual consciousness. With this belief, One is able to create a differential shift within the perceived variables of an imagined reality where anything is able to be manifested from the future into the present moment now.

To put it in simpler terms:

- believe what One imagines
- attract what One believes
- manifest what One attracts now.

Realise that everything takes time. Learn to be patient as One manifests One's belief in this world. The universe responds to One's whole of life belief or living vibrational energy, not a single word, thought or spoken affirmation. Mind–body–spirit harmony and intentional action without expectation are everything in this world.

Dr Wayne Dwyer says:

> The only limits you have are the limits you believe.

One's spirit is a 'conscious change engine' for transmuting, transforming and transcending all energy in the world. One is also an inter-dimensional Being capable of faster-than-light travel across the universe and being present in this or any other known timeline. Know that pure consciousness does not think or operate in terms of killing or healing, only in terms of navigating and recreating the observable relationships within its sphere of influence.

People, the world and Earth may appear to be broken, but it is not fixed in the past, only in the present. One is unable to go back in time, so One must learn how to best co-create a new life now. To reconfigure or shape the future to benefit all, One needs to act in alignment with One's spirit and the universe.

One exists now and it is One's time to rise and fulfil One's destiny in life. Do what must be done without expecting anything in return for oneself. Become the hero of One's life and everything that One chooses to be in this moment. Stand tall amongst the many leaders that have already been, currently are and are yet to be in this world. It is time One takes One's place as the magnificent 'Bright' that One is.

One will always be free – One is forever now.

Fusion of interstellar ideas, imagination and intelligence

Albert Einstein says:

> Given the millions of billions of Earth-like planets, life elsewhere in the universe without a doubt, does exist. In the vastness of the universe we are not alone.

It is a reasonable and rational assumption, especially given the large amount of circumstantial and 'hard evidence' of unexplained aeronautical phenomena (UAP) or unidentified flying objects (UFO), that interstellar visitors have indeed visited and are currently visiting Earth now.

Earth and its human inhabitants are, by the universe's standards, very young. It is likely that there are other Earth-like planetary civilisations in the Milky Way galaxy that are thousands or even millions of years more advanced in interactive technologies, planetary governance and spiritual consciousness. To these advanced civilisations who may be observing Earth, the human species would seem very primitive. Even though there have been great technical advances in the last hundred or so years in the areas of information technologies (computers, the internet, mobile phones, etc.), atomic weapons, DNA decoding, preventative medicine, quantum mechanics and space exploration. It is important to note that war and conflict still rage in pockets of areas on the planet, along with starvation, disease, global pandemic, hunger and poverty through the enabling of egocentric elite people's personal agendas, profit processes and political policies. Individual modern world governments have a high threshold for allowing these events to occur unchecked or without regard to the human population of the planet. This is because most governing bodies do not see or embrace the 'One world', 'One people' or 'One consciousness' concept that is the basis for One's planetary responsibility to all of humanity and future generations. Most people and leaders believe that all One is here for is to 'survive', 'look after oneself' and 'live now' without any regard, consideration or compassion for anyone else in the world or on Earth. These are the symptoms of an egoic mind that is focused on separation, power, control, greed, selfishness and living with the mindset of 'what is mine is mine and what is yours is mine too'. This is all part of a 'full spectrum dominance' vision that has been nurtured over decades within the minds of these egoic-centred sociopaths.

It is no surprise that most humans over the last few thousand years on the planet have been unwittingly and unconsciously caught up in a perpetuating egoic cycle of personal self-sabotage, corporate corruption and greed-based governance. What humanity chose to attract was a direct correlation to what was in the egoic minds of the leaders of the day. This is the legacy that has been handed down to the next generation. It is the poison chalice that has been given to the young to sip out of and it was all done in the name of 'King or Queen,

God and Country' or for 'freedom and liberty'. These are the intergenerational wounds that are still bleeding on the ground and are desperately in need of significant healing and self-love.

On the surface, it may appear that things are somewhat challenging or in chaos, but have faith and believe as One does. Trust the universe, One's spirit and oneself that everything will all work out okay – because it will.

Know that it is all part of the spiritual evolution of the human species on Earth.

It does not matter what the elite egoic people or multinational corporations do or not do – it will not stop 'the awakening' process of human consciousness on the planet. Many will try and hold on to power but it will eventually slip away like grains of sand through One's fingers. The more One tries to resist this change, the more One will become a victim of One's own egoic thoughts, ideas, habits and lifestyle. It is inevitable that egoic minds will try to destroy oneself and others in the process of change, because the alternative is too incomprehensible to imagine living. People with egoic minds will try to use all of One's influence to insist that the current social order, structure and socio-cultural doctrine must be maintained at all costs. These people will insist that any deviation to an alternative pathway will cause a major meltdown or destruction of the fabric of society itself. Anyone who proposes to shift to an alternative human/planetary operating system or higher level of consciousness will be socially isolated or personally attacked to destroy One's individual reputation and credibility. Egoic minds will do any and all things to hide the truth of One's spiritual consciousness and the fact that One is not alone in the universe. The only thing that an egoic person cares about in the world is to feed One's own ego.

As One becomes aware of One's own ego, One will be able to awaken to all the other sentient Beings on Earth whose minds are still trapped within the ego matrix. It is the function of an egoic mind to entrap, enslave and entangle others within One's illusion, like a virus infecting another host. It is not until One is able to develop a virtual egoic antivirus that can detect One's own egoic thought patterns. One can then purge it from One's mental operating system within One's mind.

Advanced civilisations will most likely be comprised of humanoid-like Beings with a higher level of consciousness and more highly developed minds that have been created as a result of an aligned conscious destiny, not egregious conflicts. The next step along the path of evolution for humanity on the planet is entering the spiritual gateway of consciousness within oneself. It is seeing and realising the illusion of reality for what it is and rising above it to a more profound way of thinking, working, living and being on Earth. There is nowhere to hide from this change and nowhere to run that will not be influenced by these planetary changes in consciousness. Everyone will be affected by this conscious wave of change.

A side effect of this change will be the adaptation of the brain due to its neuroplasticity. In essence, One will eventually develop new neural pathways in the brain and create new connections that will give rise to new thoughts, ideas and understandings about oneself and the world in which One lives now. In some people, this will happen gradually; in others, it will happen almost instantaneously. Just take a deep breath. This is all part of the evolving process on planet Earth as a sentient Being of the universe.

Interstellar Beings' intuitive intelligence and innovative technologies will be beyond what humanity can handle at this point in time, because it will not be ego-based or ego-centric. Advanced civilisations that are founded on an 'awakened consciousness' and state-based existence in the universe have no need for war, conflict, hate, jealousy, separation, control, greed, power or selfishness. These civilisations will be:

- Type 1, 2 or 3 spiritually based civilisations
- created out of a shared consciousness or state-based culture and interstellar lifestyle

- completely aligned to the concept of one world, one people, one conscious existence based on harmony, balanced and peaceful co-existence with the planet as well as all life on it, where population is a function of intelligent design and not egoic desire
- capable of interstellar travel and exploration of the galaxy using gravity wave 'attraction' or faster-than-light, state-based driving force systems.
- able to master zero-point energy, also known as ground state energy
- extremely skilled and very efficient in managing inner states of consciousness, consciousness projection and telepathic communication.
- highly competent at 3D atomic printing in the production of programmable matter and new combinational alloys for on and off-world (in space) construction.
- adept and highly accomplished in understanding the inherent skills of using 'quantum consciousness' as a way of interfacing, managing and manipulating the world and everything in it as well as creating new bio-nano artificial intelligence.
- employ seamless integration or psycho-techno-eco fusion of living 'humanoid' consciousness, interstellar technologies and biological ecology
- a living expression of One's shared consciousness and inter-connectedness (individual, family, social, community and planetary) awareness that co-creates a new spiritual interstellar reality of the future.

Let us for a moment have a look at the issue of gravity and how it relates to One's life and lifestyle on Earth. Without gravity, life on Earth would simply not be possible. It is essential for the evolution of all species, including humans. But what if One could manipulate gravity using some form of advanced interstellar technology? It would revolutionise the way people think, live and work on the planet, just as electricity affected society and changed how people lived in the late 1800s.

The hypothesis is:

> The wave state of gravity is probable relative to its relationship within the field in which it exists. This means that gravity is a constant when the relationship is fixed. However, if the gravity field is altered due to a differential anomaly or wave within the field, this wave will alter the effects of the gravity field and all things within it, causing the gravity field to bend, shift and transform in direct proportion to the wave state having an effect upon it.

The only thing widely known that produces gravity is mass; however, this will change with the fusion of interstellar knowledge, technologies and consciousness. This process is already happening on Earth. It also coincides with the 'awakening' of all sentient Beings to One's higher level of consciousness.

Previously, most scientific minds believed that gravity was fixed, but it is not. The same principle also applies to consciousness. Consciousness is not fixed; it is state-based and creates its own multi-non-dimensional states in which it operates and affects the universe. This is the paradigm shift that One needs to come to terms with now to transcend One's current thinking, living and being on the planet.

Conscious evolution on Earth

The conscious evolution of humanity is not to be feared; it is to be embraced and celebrated. It will, however, require people to let go of One's old life in order to live a new life on Earth. Do not fear, it is all part of 'the awakening' process of One's higher spiritual self. As part of this inner change, One will naturally upload a new and improved human living operating system within One's mind. Initially, it may indeed challenge One's comfort zone, belief system and current sense of direction. In some cases, it will most likely impact One's existing relationships and friendship circle. Other side effects of this change may include social isolation, not being liked or understood as well as being labelled wacky, weird or eccentric. This is a result of One shifting One's vibrational energy to a higher level of consciousness, which is effectively out of alignment with the status quo in society at this moment.

One will also notice other anomalies, such as a disentanglement from social drama, thought processes becoming heightened or clear, increased ability to sense situations and people more accurately with respect to One's feelings and intentions. One will also begin to become disengaged with society while remaining present in the moment. It may seem strange at first, but trust the process. The benefits of this inner shift in awareness will be completely overwhelming in One's life. Know that with this change, One will feel a tremendous sense of inner joy and alignment with the universe or Source Consciousness itself. One will value freedom of thought, freedom of speech, freedom of association and freedom of existence at a significantly higher level than ever before in One's life.

It does not matter what others think, do, feel or say – One is on One's way to living a new life, with a new purpose and creating new outcomes in the world. It may feel like One is starting all over again and, to some extent, this is true. But have faith that everything will work out, because it will.

Moving forward with One's life, One will begin to see incremental changes in the way One thinks, the way One responds to situations, people and the way One is able to influence the space-time reality within One's living presence. As One steps into this unknown space, the synergy of intentional thoughts will begin to synchronise almost instantaneously. Whatever One is thinking about seems to come to or be attracted to One in an effortless way. This is in direct proportion to how One is affecting the non-dimensional field of consciousness in which One exists now. Nothing is what it seems and the things which seem to be real are simply a projection within the illusion of reality.

This will be a weird concept at first, but as time goes by, One will become less and less concerned with the idea and more focused on 'being within it' or 'staying in the moment'. One will be able to transcend time and space itself and skip consciously across the universe and return. One will be able to increase One's conscious awareness in all directions, which will lead to additional awakening moments of insight and profound understandings in the world. One's level of intuitive knowing of things will increase dramatically as One is able to let go of One's preformatted egoic thoughts and purge all negative memes and energy from One's human form. After all, One's human form is simply a quantum system and, by the simple act of observing it, One has the ability to significantly change it. This change in consciousness will also affect One's human form in ways that One will not be able to precisely predict or foresee. Be patient and be guided by One's spirit, intuitive intelligence and universe along 'the way'.

Creating this new or altered state of consciousness within oneself will enable a new living vibrational energy that will attract new people who are meant for One. These people including interstellar visitors are going to meet One on the other side of this change process. Not everyone who was once One's friend before this paradigm shift will continue to be One's friend in the future. As One moves forward in the moment, One will be initialising a new comfort zone or state-based awareness around the things that One is spiritually and consciously aligned to now. One's inner light, love and oneness will be seen even brighter than ever before. In losing One's old self, One will be co-creating a new divine identity that is vastly more aligned with One's spirit and the universe.

Carl Jung says:

> People will do anything, no matter how absurd, in order to avoid facing their own souls [spirits]. One does not become enlightened by imagining figures of light, but by making the darkness conscious.

As more and more people on the planet awaken to One's inner higher self and spiritual consciousness, the whole vibration of the Earth will change. This will also have an effect on the gravity field and non-dimensional states of existence for everyone.

A time is fast approaching when all of humanity will reach a tipping point of aligned consciousness. This tipping point on the planet only requires approximately one per cent of humanity to be in alignment to significantly influence everyone else. At this moment, things will begin to dramatically shift in a positive way. It is not possible to predict the exact time, but it is probable that this moment is a known certainty. What is known is that a wave of spiritual consciousness will move silently and effortlessly around the planet, influencing people in a way that has never been done before. It will alter One's current thought patterns, memes and spiritual awareness. This will then have a cascading and flow-on effect on the everyday lives of people, communities, societies, First Nations and nation states around the world.

It will eventually change how One sees oneself and One's place in the world, on planet Earth and in the universe. Some people will be very scared of this change at first, and may try and hide from it. Others will embrace it with open arms.

There are many 'true believers' in this world who require no evidence of this coming change of consciousness on Earth. There are also numerous sceptics that will require evidence before One even begins to consider the possibility of change. By 'true believers', One is referring to people who already have an inner belief and knowingness in One's spirit and not people of a particular faith-based religion. All religions are an interpretation of a spiritual experience for the purpose of affirming a particular religious practice in order to maintain a position of authority and power over people. All religions dilute the truth of One's own spiritual existence in this world. Spirit, soul or cosmic consciousness exists within One now. Religion is the applied practice to attain a particular spiritual validation or to be deemed worthy by a higher power or supreme Being in the universe, but One is capable of directly accessing One's spirit without being subject to social order, holy rules or sacred hierarchy.

It does not matter if One is a 'true believer' or not, because this wave of consciousness is already being formed and in the process of being present in the lives of people now.

A consciousness shift or altered inner awareness will happen either by individual self-awakening processes within One or shared collective awareness. It will also happen through the natural synergy and aligned resonance of simply living on Earth. It may even happen or be triggered by shared news feeds or information on multiple shared media platforms on the internet. It will be instantaneous, sudden and unexpected in most cases.

The more people with egoic minds try to take control of this inevitable change on the planet, the more this will quicken the pace of the awakening process. In fact, without even realising it, the egoic elites of this world, ego-centric corporate world order and geo-political world governance systems have already lost. What is not certain is by how much and to what extent. One is unable to stop the tide of change, as it changes all in its path.

A change in human consciousness is on the horizon and it is here now. It is in both places at the same time, just like state-based theory or quantum mechanics. Another way of looking at it is to think of oneself as a state-based system of individual consciousness affecting another state-based system of collective consciousness through the simple process of observation. Everything that One looks at changes because of the simple act of looking at it from the same non-dimensional state of existence. This principle applies equally to the human world and the quantum realm. Individual and collective change is both a function of applied intentional action and direct observation. This means that by using One's consciousness, One is able to effect change simply by focusing One's spiritual awareness on it. It is an incredible thing to realise that One has the capacity to influence great positive changes in the world through mindful meditation.

There are many things that One can do to support oneself in manifesting a new Earth and life on the planet. There is also a groundswell of interest in shifting the energy of the people on the planet to a higher level of consciousness in order to transcend Earth's current issues, concerns and worries.

Einstein says:

> We cannot solve our problems with the same thinking we used when we created them.

One needs to shift both One's thought processes and One's frame of reference. This is why it is critical for humanity to awaken to a higher level of consciousness and inner awareness in the world. One will require a new way of thinking or consciousness framework to move everyone beyond this point in time now. The old thoughts and thinking have gotten people here, but will not get everyone to where One needs to go in the future.

Those people who are entirely focused on living a life that is mind-based thinking will struggle to accept a state-based life of existence. Most of these people will not be aware of One's own spirit, soul or cosmic consciousness and refuse to entertain the idea of One's divine presence in the world. But with time, One will begin to realise the co-existence of mind–body and spirit.

Breaking with traditional thought patterns and long-held established doctrines of deterministic thinking of the past will not be easy. It will require a global paradigm shift in both thinking and consciousness. Even though this call to action is globally significant, it can and will happen on Earth. The awakening resonance of the planet and the people on it is collectively increasing each and every day. There are signs all around One. Just be open minded and it will come to One. Everything is already in play. As One attracts a new conscious future, this new manifested reality is being attracted to One now.

Paradox of spiritual existence

It is important that One discusses spiritual consciousness in greater detail and also provide more context as it relates to the world in which One lives. Let's take a deep dive into the simple complexities that appear as One considers the heart of spiritual consciousness. Consciousness is as simple as it is complex. The more One is able to free and open One's mind, the more One will be able to become present with One's intuitive intelligence and know the secrets of the universe. Be patient and all will be revealed to One right on time. The universe has its own way of working everything out in synchronicity with all things in life. Believe in the universe – trust the process.

One of the great problems or challenges is that modern science is built upon determinism and the ability to predict things. In most cases, the observable physical or material world works like this. However, Newtonian laws of motion, standing physics principles, constants in well-known equations and theories, which are all based on determinism, are useless when talking about quantum physics or spiritual consciousness.

One needs a different way of thinking about the sub-atomic realm and non-dimensional states of spiritual consciousness in order to make sense of it, as these do not operate the same way in a macro world. Eckhart Tolle says:

> The most vital thing in spiritual life is to be able to watch your mind – to be the observer of your mind – so that the mind is not controlling you.

As discussed in previous chapters, One as a sentient Being of the universe has seven individual states of consciousness within One's divine consciousness:

1. Knowing
2. Awareness
3. Oneness
4. Joy
5. Free will
6. Peace
7. Presence

The eighth state is a fusion of all states: One's complete or whole divine spiritual consciousness.

As a spiritual Being, once One is in a particular state of spiritual consciousness (as a function of aligned intention) the probability of a Being's state of consciousness is determined by the square of One's consciousness, which is represented here by the omega symbol (Ω) from the Greek alphabet, meaning the end of something, or the last/final/ultimate limit of it. It also symbolises something great, or the end of an increment of great development. This increment could be the universe, the planet, a country or even an individual.

Therefore, One's infinite existence in the universe can be represented by the following equation:

Infinite Existence = Infinity × Consciousness²
$IE = \infty \times \Omega^2$

However, the uncertainty principle in quantum physics says that the momentum and position of a particle cannot both be precisely determined at the same time. This also applies to spiritual consciousness, so is not possible to accurately predict a specific state of consciousness of any spiritual Being. All One can do is predict the probabilities of existing in one or all seven infinite states of consciousness simultaneously.

This can be represented by the numerical value of 5,041 probable states of consciousness at any moment. This value is calculated on every individual single state × every multiple state × all states of existence ($1 \times 2 \times 3 \times 4 \times 5 \times 6 \times 7 + n$, where $n = 1$).

The surprising consequence of this fact is that, until a state is actualised within a spiritual Being, One's consciousness essentially exists in all states! This is the paradox of spiritual consciousness.

There is no way of knowing whether a Being's consciousness is in a particular state until One intentionally aligns to this state of existence. So, according to the infinite state theory of spiritual consciousness, until One is in alignment, One is in any single state and all states simultaneously! This is the fundamental paradox presented by the theory. It is a way of guiding One's mind to think about One's infinite existence as multi-non-dimensional conscious states. Until the state of spiritual consciousness is intentionally aligned within a sentient Being, One exists in all states at the same time.

What this means is that, as spirit, soul or cosmic consciousness, One does not exist in a single state of consciousness to the exclusion of all the other states. One is a multi-state Being capable of existing in one or more states all at the same time. This may seem too incredible to be true, but just sit with this concept of existence for a moment. The more One comes to realise that One as spirit is not just a single thing, the more One will be able to grasp the greatness of One's Being in the universe.

This idea of living a state-based existence in the universe is only the beginning. Statum intuitanics (state-based knowing, sensing, or understanding by intuition and/or intuitive spiritual intelligence) is the spiritual equivalent of quantum mechanics. It allows One to instantaneously shift between one and all states of spiritual existence, move through a field of dimensional reality (i.e. altered consciousness) beyond the speed of light with zero resistance, and align in complete synchronicity with other spiritual Beings in another part of the solar system, galaxy or universe. This is the phenomenon known as spiritual entanglement. This will one day revolutionise the way people think, live, work and be on Earth as well as this solar system. This type of human paradigm shift will lay the foundation for an interstellar, spiritually based Type 1 civilisation on the planet, advance spiritual consciousness and create a fusion of interstellar technologies that will underpin the exploration of the galaxy and known universe. A day is fast approaching when a belief arises that will show a significant non-dimensional correlation and relationship between Source Consciousness (human or individual consciousness) and quantum consciousness.

Einstein says:

> Everyone who is seriously involved in the pursuit of science becomes convinced that a spirit is manifest in the laws of the Universe – a spirit vastly superior to that of man, and one in the face of which we with our modest powers must feel humble.

As One comes to terms with the realisation that One is not human, not One's human body and not One's human thoughts, One will open an infinite chasm in One's life to explore One's spiritual consciousness. This truth will become undeniable as One is drawn closer to the process of self-realisation and self-awakening. It is like riding a cosmic wave of spiritual gravity home to Source. It will naturally attract One to the centrepoint of One's existence in the universe.

Do not resist what One has known all along. Choose simply to embrace oneself as a spiritual Being and interstellar traveller. One's divinity is not linked to or grounded in any planet, solar system or galaxy in the universe. One is so much more than this. The origin of One's infinite existence is not in question, because One already knows the answer.

One Exists – so One is.

It is time to step into the light of One's Being and become the 'Bright' that One is and was always meant to be on Earth. Do not be fooled, tricked or trapped by One's ego into thinking that the illusions of the material world are One's reality. It is simply a way to explore, express and experience One's spiritual consciousness in the universe along with all other sentient Beings.

The more One is able to see the truth of One's divine existence, the more One will be able to realise that:

- Everything is connected – all is one.
- All things change, nothing is permanent.
- Everything is energy and vibrating as part of the duality of the cosmos.
- Patterns repeat in synchronicity throughout the universe.
- Everything that happens is to support One's higher self through vibrational attraction – it is all relative.
- One is part of everything and everything is within One.
- One's infinite existence is as a multi-non-dimensional state-based consciousness or sentient Being in the universe.

Carl Jung says:

> What you most need will be found where you least want to look.

There is nothing more important to true personal growth and inner awareness than realising who One is now. Take the time to look inside oneself and align with One's inner spirit. This is where One needs to shine a light so One can awaken and see clearly in the world today. One's inner path is the way to One's outer journey in life. One simple step at a time, One simple moment of inner realisation and One great awakening for all of humanity on Earth.

One's ability to make a positive impact in One's life and the world depends on how much One is able to let go of One's ego and egoic fears and become aligned with the way of the universe. One's greatest fear is not the darkness, self-limiting beliefs or negative energy within One. It is One's divine light, oneness and pure positive energy to be all that One can be in this world. This is where One's greatest potential exists. One's spiritual consciousness and 'light energy' to be true to One's higher spiritual self is being diminished and distorted through egoic limiting beliefs and thoughts within One's mind. When One is able to review, release, and replace this conditioned belief system and thinking patterns with state-based awareness, something amazing starts to happen almost instantly. One begins to naturally and effortlessly align to One's states of consciousness within One's spirit and expand One's divine presence exponentially. One will then be able to open new gateway experiences to live life from a higher state of existence on the planet.

One way of thinking about things is that these changes could be seen as One's own personal superpowers, if this means being in alignment with One's higher self and intuitive intelligence. Other benefits of being an 'awake' or 'conscious' person will include a higher level of perception, awareness and knowing. With practice and guidance, One will have heightened senses in these areas and be able to 'tap into' a state of non-dimensional consciousness beyond space and time. One's possible experiences are endless. One will significantly increase One's capacity to navigate new paths in life because One will be able to imagine a future reality and manifest it in the present. One does this by making a conscious choice to attract it into One's life experiences by creating an aligned destiny. Essentially, One will create a consciousness wave to distort the fabric of space-time so that One is attracted to this new reality and this new reality is attracted to One. This process will occur in a synchronous way as if it is meant to be because it already exists now.

To the universe, all reality is virtual.

This may sound too good to be true, but trust One – it works.

Once One has shifted One's mind to state-based thinking, things will flow freely in a way that will align with the harmonic vibrations of nature and natural rhythmic patterns of the universe. One is an incredible spirit with powers beyond measure. One has the inherent ability to influence the fabric of space-time or the dimensional field of altered consciousness.

To be fully present in the moment as an indomitable spirit with limitless potential is to simultaneously express all of One's infinite existence as spirit, soul or cosmic consciousness in this world and universe. What One does next will shape the destiny of humanity on Earth, in this solar system and galaxy.

Infinite Existence

The following is an equation for One's infinite existence in the universe. The probability of a Being's state of consciousness is determined by the square of One's consciousness, which is represented here by the omega symbol (Ω) from the Greek alphabet. One's infinite existence in the universe can be represented by the following equation:

$$\text{Infinite Existence} = \text{Infinity} \times \text{Consciousness}^2$$
$$IE = \infty\, \Omega^2$$

Living One's inner way now

Suggestions for putting the learnings, teachings and pointings of this chapter into practice in One's daily life:

- Understand that the next step along the path of evolution for humanity on the planet is entering the spiritual gateway of consciousness within oneself.
- Realise that egoic minds will do any and all things to hide the truth of One's spiritual consciousness and the fact that One is not alone in the universe.
- What is certain is that a change in human consciousness is on the horizon and it is here now.
- Realise that consciousness is not fixed, it is state-based and creates its own multi-non-dimensional state in which it operates and affects the universe.
- Think about One's infinite existence as a field of multi-non-dimensional conscious states.
- Know that to the universe, all reality is virtual.
- Learn how to shift One's mind to state-based thinking, so things flow freely in a way that will align with the harmonic vibrations of nature and natural rhythmic patterns of the universe.

Acknowledgements

Thanks to everyone who enjoyed the books *One*, *Two*, *Three* and *Awaken*. One is grateful for the opportunity to bring these books to the world and help people on One's personal journey of self-reflection, self-realisation and self-awakening.

Infinite Existence has been a deep dive into exploring that which resonates within One's mind, body and spirit.

One acknowledges everyone who has been part of this personal journey and shared experience to raise the collective vibration of human consciousness on the planet now and in the future.

It is with great humility and honour that One wishes to acknowledge all the great spiritual teachers, thinkers and Masters who have committed to a life of sharing what One knows to be part of the essence of One's own inner truth. In doing so, One becomes a reflection of the divine Source, the Creator, God, Allah or the universe itself.

These luminaries include such notable persons as Mooji, Eckhart Tolle, Thich Nhat Hanh, Dr Deepak Chopra, Dr Wayne Dyer, Ram Dass, Louise Hay, Doreen Virtue, Allan Watts, Stephen Covey, William Glasser, Carl Jung, His Holiness the Dalai Lama, Buddha, Osho, Rumi, Marianne Williamson, Joseph Campbell, Mahatma Gandhi, Lao Tzu and various Buddhist teachers, Zen Masters and many other First Nations leaders, including One's mother, Shirley Foley née Wondunna.

This book is a way of sharing One's teachings, learnings, pointings and powerful mindful practices that allow One to stop limiting thoughts, beliefs and behaviours and start experiencing an aligned life that is manifested in the present moment and centred within One's spirit, soul or cosmic consciousness.

One is grateful to all the readers of this book, for whom this journey has been a transformative process along the path of spiritual inspiration, conscious awakening and divine alignment within oneself.

May an inner way of peace, prosperity, abundance and contentment be realised and awakened within One now.

Endnote

Co-existence theory of the universe suggests that all dimensional matter-energy (altered consciousness) and non-dimensional states (consciousness) or field-states co-exist relative to each other. As a theory of everything, it describes the coherence of all separate theories into a single theory of co-existence within the universe. It is a theory that gives rise to a singularity of infinite existence.

What this means is that, while fields and states are observed as separate functions of the universe, these two different perceived realities indeed co-exist as One or part of the whole. One realises that One cannot use the same ideas, concepts, principles, equations or language to describe field-based matter and energy in the macro world in the same way that One would describe state-based particles and movement in the quantum realm or spiritual consciousness. The same also applies when One is talking about state-based conscious existence.

In simple terms, when thinking about the three-dimensional world, One needs to use a particular set of ideas, concepts and language to refer to tangible things like mass, position and velocity. When thinking about the non-dimensional realm – for example, quantum mechanics or spiritual consciousness – One needs to use another set of ideas, concepts and language to refer to the intangible states of things, like quantum state or states of consciousness.

This may sound a little complicated or may even put One's head in a bit of a spin. But think of it like this: the way co-existence works in the universe is like a field within a state within a field within a state, and so on and so forth. The most familiar example is the human body. The human body is universally accepted as being made up of mind–body and spirit (consciousness). The physical or tangible mind–body (dimensional field) co-exists within an intangible consciousness (non-dimensional state). One's human form (field-state co-existence) also co-exists within the world (next level dimensional field). The world co-exists within an intangible Source Consciousness (next level non-dimensional state).

In conclusion, it is all about shifting One's thinking to realise that all people co-exist as a field within a state of individual existence, which also resides within another field-state of collective existence. All types of co-existence give rise to other probable field-states of existence in the universe.

An alternative way to think about it is like unwrapping an endless gift. Imagine for a moment that there is an incredibly large, transparent, empty balloon, ball or sphere with a single large black box inside it. If One were able to 'teleport' oneself inside this sphere and then look inside this black box, One would find an infinite number of smaller transparent spheres, each containing its own small black box. If One selected a small sphere and 'teleported' oneself inside so that One could open the small black box, One would discover that this small black box was filled with an infinite number of tiny transparent spheres, again with its own tiny black box within it ... so on and so forth. This is a model for the continuity of infinite co-existence.

Therefore, as spirit, soul or cosmic consciousness, which is host to a human form, One co-exists within a single field-state of existence while simultaneously co-existing with other human beings or life forms on Earth of similar, same or like field-states of existence within the infinite continuity of probable field-states in the universe.

This allows for the infinite number of combinations of life co-existing with other life as expressed within the natural order of the universe. Therefore, diversity in all its forms is a natural function of the expression of the universe itself.

Einstein says:

The measure of intelligence is the ability to change.

Shifting One's thinking to a higher level of consciousness changes One's relationship with oneself, people, interstellar Beings and the world completely. One can see more clearly, align with One's spirit more deeply and observe the world from a spiritual perspective with greater intuitive intelligence and cosmic wisdom. With this evolution of One's inner consciousness, One will awaken to One's divinity, spiritual sovereignty and align with 'the way' of the universe. One's way to be all that One can be now is a matter of conscious choice, co-creative intention and aligned destiny.

Anything is possible and everything is probable in the universe.

Field-state model of co-existence

Other books by Shawn Wondunna-Foley

One, Two and Three
Mindful spiritual quotes to inspire one to live
a prosperous, abundant and awakened life

Spirit Language Guide

Awaken: One people,
one planet, one spirit:
Co-create the best version
of oneself now

All titles available from innerway.com.au

www.ingramcontent.com/pod-product-compliance
Lightning Source LLC
Chambersburg PA
CBHW020318010526
44107CB00054B/1884